A History of Vocational and Career Education in Ohio: 1828-2000

A History of Vocational and Career Education in Ohio: 1828-2000

Byrl R. Shoemaker & Darrell L. Parks

iUniverse, Inc.
New York Lincoln Shanghai

A History of Vocational and Career Education in Ohio: 1828-2000

iUniverse books may be ordered through booksellers or by contacting:

iUniverse
2021 Pine Lake Road, Suite 100
Lincoln, NE 68512
www.iuniverse.com
1-800-Authors (1-800-288-4677)

The views expressed in this work are solely those of the author and do not necessarily reflect the views of the publisher, and the publisher hereby disclaims any responsibility for them.

ISBN: 978-0-595-42497-9 (pbk)
ISBN: 978-0-595-87144-5 (cloth)

Printed in the United States of America

Contents

Acknowledgments

Compiling a history of vocational education in Ohio was no small task. Important documents that would have been invaluable could not be located or have been lost over time. Much of the information included in this publication had never been recorded but was based on recall of various individuals who lived through the times.

Appreciation and gratitude is expressed to all of those who contributed to make this history a reality, especially those groups and individuals that made financial contributions toward the completion of this project, including the Ohio Association of Career and Technical Education affiliates—Career-based Intervention, Ohio Career Technical Administrators, Affiliation of Tech Prep Academics, T&I Education, Special Needs and Health Careers and Technology, and to Mett's Educational Products.

Special thanks go to all of the contributing authors who added that touch of authenticity and who, quite frankly, were sole possessors of much of the information that they wrote. Had some of the information collected for this document not been collected when it was, it would have been lost forever as evidenced by the untimely deaths of Robert Balthaser and Harry Davis.

Thanks is also extended to everyone who so graciously responded to requests for information or who went on the search for missing information that added to the legitimacy of this chronicle. And thanks to Becky Parker and Jim Pinchak for their careful reading of drafts and making comments that enhanced the internal consistency, accuracy and readability of the text.

And finally, thanks to Scott Aiken, journalist and public relations counselor, for his sage advice in formatting the final copy and exploring publication options to make the history available to all interested readers.

Introduction

As history goes, vocational education covers a relatively recent period of time. However, the roots of vocational education go back to the beginning of mankind. Fathers and mothers have always transmitted the skills and knowledge of their culture to their children in order to teach them to survive; each new generation added something to the total of skills and knowledge. Work to sustain the family's existence, and the care of children and the home were basic to the continuation of the species. These functions consumed about all of a family's waking hours. The picture of the Native American man showing his young son how to make an arrow is a fairly modern example of vocational education.

As the work of the father moved from the farm to work for an employer or for a business serving other persons, it became more difficult for the children to learn how to make a living. When the business was family-owned, boys followed the craft of their fathers, and mothers taught their daughters the skills of the home. In this period of time, children were frequently indentured to an employer, often at no wages or very meager earnings, to learn the skills of an occupation. This practice was the forerunner of today's apprenticeship system. In today's apprenticeship program, the learner is paid a training wage and is taught the skills of an occupation over a specified period of time.

With the advent of the industrial revolution and mass production, the father was no longer able to impart the skills of work to his children. With the introduction of women to work outside the home, opportunities for the mother to transmit the skills of homemaking to her daughter/s also diminished. There was a growing void in the transmission of the skills for economic survival and for homemaking.

Our nation recognized that educating youth to be good citizens was necessary for the survival of our republic, thus the initiation of the common schools. The system started with the elementary school, and was gradually extended to the high school. In 1910 the Carnegie Foundation conducted a study to establish the basis for a high school curriculum to prepare youth for entrance into a university. Since almost all young people who completed high school went on to college, the proposed curriculum focused on the academics that were important for college admission. Four "solid" subjects composed the core of the curriculum—English, history, mathematics, and science. In 1910, Henry Ford was producing the fabulous Model T car. Today, automobiles are far more advanced, but our educational system still focuses on the same subjects taught as isolated bodies of knowledge.

As a society, we are still concerned about preparing all youth to go to college; yet only 20% of the jobs require a bachelor's degree. Our focus in public education is open to question. Educating our youth and adults to participate in life as responsible citizens, to lead disciplined lives and respect the rights of others, and to prepare for work, other than the professions, still are not major priorities of the majority of business leaders, politicians or educators.

This history is about a program that can be described as follows: The primary purpose of vocational education is to equip persons for gainful employment. The program serves the needs of two distinct groups. First, are the adults who are already in the work force; second, are the young people and adults who are preparing to enter occupations that require something less than a college degree. These occupations are primarily in the fields of agriculture and natural resources, business and information technology, distribution and sales, family and consumer sciences, health, and trades and industry.

Throughout this publication, the reader will note that the authors use *vocational education* and *career and technical education* interchangeably; however, the terms mean the same thing. In the main, in the program's evolution, it took on the name of the federal legislation that provided federal dollars to support the movement. Thus the *Smith Hughes Act*, the *Vocational Education Act of 1963*, and the *Vocational Education Amendments of 1968 and 1976* established a national nomenclature of vocational education. Then in the 1990s, the *Carl D. Perkins Vocational and Technical Education Act of 1998* (P.L. 105-332) was enacted and subsequent federal legislation continued to use the term *technical education*. Thus, over time, the term *vocational education,* thought by many to be somewhat narrow and delimiting, has given way to a more relevant moniker, *career and technical education.* And on occasion, the reader might note a text reference to *career/technical and adult education (CTAE)* as a more inclusive descriptor of a program that serves both secondary and postsecondary clientele.

Vocational education gives purpose and meaning to education by relating knowledge and skills to the world of work. Vocational education provides the technical knowledge, work skills, and problem-solving capabilities necessary for employment. Yet, it goes beyond training for job skills. It develops critical thinking skills, attitudes, and work habits that contribute to a satisfying and productive life.

Vocational education also contributes to the general education needs of youth, such as citizenship, respect for others, and acceptance of personal responsibility. Its unique contribution is, however, in preparing people for work. It is a part of a well-rounded program of studies aimed at developing highly skilled and efficient workers. It recognizes that American workers must be competent—economically, socially, emotionally, physically, and in a civic sense.

Dr. Darrell Parks wrote the history of vocational education in Ohio up to 1940, as well as the period from 1983 to 2000. Dr. Byrl Shoemaker wrote the history for the four decades from 1940 to his retirement as state director of career and technical education in 1982. Contributing authors for Chapter VII also included former assistant directors Robert Balthaser, Dr. Bernard Nye, Sonia Cole Price, and Harry Davis. Chapter VIII was authored by former Associate Director Dr. G. James Pinchak.

Vocational education programs grew rapidly from 1963 through 1983. From 1983 to the present, efforts have concentrated on improving and modifying programs in response to the ever-changing needs of a highly skilled workforce.

Ohio was the first state in the nation in which all youth had access to an adequate program of vocational education. Ohio was also unique in its use of the facilities to serve adults. In fact, more adults than teenagers are enrolled in vocational education courses in Ohio. This history also records the birth of the two-year technical institutes. Most of these institutes, now coordinated by the Ohio Board of Regents, have become community and state colleges that prepare technicians and paraprofessionals for business and industry, and provide the first two years of a baccalaureate degree for a large number of students.

Impetus for the major developments in vocational education came from the State Department of Education. The State Board of Education, the State Superintendent of Public Instruction, and the Division of Vocational Education staff provided excellent leadership to create a broad career and technical education program for all Ohio youth and adults.

Still, the efforts would have been in vain without the support of Gov. James A. Rhodes, along with strong, bipartisan support from members of the Ohio General Assembly. Ohio voters also voted their local shares of the money required to develop vocational and technical education throughout the state.

Finally, as Howard Mansfield noted, history is an imperfect record, at best an approximation skewed by transient passions and by the eccentric spin of competing events. Some things small receive disproportionate attention. Some things great are lost forever.

1

The Formative Years

✦

1828-1939

The history of vocational education in Ohio reflects the changing needs of Ohio's economy. Ohio followed and then led the technology-driven growth in national productivity, along with the requisite growth of worker skills. The peaks and valleys of the U.S. business cycle were amplified here. Ohio set the standard for training programs that helped workers survive the bad times and make the most of the good ones.

Because European wars made the export of raw materials highly profitable and English manufactured goods were readily available, industrialization came late to the United States. Throughout much of the 1800s, productivity in Ohio rested more on its natural resources than on any technical capabilities. Rich agricultural lands, plentiful game and a network of navigable waterways attracted traders and settlers, sparking trade throughout the New World.

Ohio's strategic geographic location made it the gateway to the west. By 1810, the state's population had reached almost 600,000. Internal and external trade prompted the building of the first national road. The Ohio River became an important waterway for transportation and commerce, and the river contributed significantly to Cincinnati becoming Ohio's largest city. Ohio railroads grew from 300 miles of track to 3,000 miles in just 10 years. In the 1850s, improved shipping made Ohio the beneficiary of Minnesota iron ore. By the turn of the century, Cleveland had become the world's largest producer of steel.

Ohio underwent a rapid industrial revolution. The presence of large coal deposits coupled with the ready access to iron ore shifted Ohio's economic center from Cincinnati to the Cleveland-Youngstown corridor. Manufacturing transformed other cities throughout the state with Akron becoming known for its rubber production, Toledo for its glass blowing, and Dayton for the manufacturing of business machines.

The industrial revolution also spawned a revolution in education. As manufacturing expanded, so did the need to educate workers with the skills essential to drive the industrialization movement. In 1870, The Ohio Agricultural and Mechanical College was founded as a land grant institution in accordance with the *Morrill Act* of 1862 and opened its doors for students in September 1873. The school was situated within a farming community on the northern edge of Columbus and was intended to matriculate students of various agricultural and mechanical disciplines. In 1878 the college's curriculum was broadened to include a more diverse spectrum of educational offerings and the institution was renamed The Ohio State University.

Most of the high schools in Ohio were built after 1865 and adopted a common curriculum of general literacy, math skills, and moral values. Then Horace Mann, the first secretary of the Massachusetts Board of Education, brought national attention to the economic value of education, calling it ... *more powerful in the production and gainful employment of the total wealth of the country than all other things mentioned in the works of the political economists.*

Even before Mann's declaration, educational leaders in Cincinnati, which was rapidly becoming the machine trades capital of the nation, recognized the need for a more formal approach to workforce education. The city established its historic Mechanics Institute in 1828.

In time, other Ohio cities followed suit. In 1875, Toledo opened a school for the promotion of knowledge in the arts and trades and related sciences. The Cleveland Manual Training School opened in 1886. Industrial arts classes were introduced at the Sullivant School and North High School in Columbus in 1894. The John H. Patterson Cooperative High School opened in Dayton in 1914, and the Akron Continuation School was founded in 1920. In addition, Elyria introduced the teaching of agriculture at the secondary level in 1902.

John W. Zeller, Ohio's chief state school officer, reinforced the utilitarian responsibility of public education in a speech to the Ohio Teachers' Association on June 29, 1910:

> *Education from now on ... must serve more effectively not only the classes but also the masses, and what our agricultural colleges have done for the select few, the high schools must now do for the many. It cannot too often be repeated that the modern high school is not the lineal descendant of the old-time academy, and its function is not to fit for college. It is a new institution, and its function is to educate its natural and local constituency for the duties of life....*

With the passage of the *Tuttle Bill* in 1907, the state legislature demonstrated its concern for workforce preparedness. The bill ... *put the subjects of agriculture, industrial, and vocational education, and trade schools before all the boards of education in the state and gave the boards the power to establish and maintain manual training and commercial departments in connection with the school system.*

Ohio was not alone in its concern for preparing and sustaining an educated workforce. Around the turn of the century, debates were taking place at the national level regarding the need for some type of vocational education. Concurrently, the National Society for the Promotion of Industrial Education was formed in New York in 1906. A similar organization was formed in the middle states, the Vocational Education Association of the Middle West (which in 1925 became part of the American Vocational Association).

Early in 1914, Congress established the Commission on National Aid to Vocational Education under the chairmanship of Senator Hoke Smith of Georgia. The commission was to study the need for vocational education and report back in June of that same year. The commission's findings resulted in the passage of the *Smith-Hughes Act of 1917*, also referred to as the *Vocational Extension Act.*

The *Smith-Hughes Act* provided federal funds for vocational education at the secondary level. To administer the program, Congress created the Federal Board of Vocational Education, comprised of the secretaries of agriculture, commerce and labor, the Commissioner of Education, and three citizens appointed by the president to represent the views of labor, manufacturing, and commerce. This federal board remained intact for nearly three decades until it was abolished in 1946. Subsequently, each state was to establish a similar board to develop a detailed plan for the use of federal vocational education dollars.

On March 30, 1917, Ohio's General Assembly passed the *Ohio Acceptance Act*, acknowledging the terms and conditions for federal aid to vocational education as set forth in the *Smith-Hughes Act*. Governor James M. Cox appointed Ohio's first State Board of Vocational Education. It included the following individuals: Dr. Randall J. Condon, Superintendent of the Cincinnati Public Schools; Walter Edmund, Superintendent of the Sandusky Public Schools; A. C. Eldredge, Assistant Superintendent of the Cleveland Public Schools; Alfred Vivian, Dean of the College of Agriculture, The Ohio State University; S. J. McClure, a hardware dealer from Brilliant, and Frank B. Pearson, State Superintendent of Public Instruction, an ex-officio member and secretary of the Board.

Ohio completed its first plan for vocational education in 1917, and the Federal Board for Vocational Education approved the plan on December 14 that same year. The plan provided for the appointment of supervisors for the three instructional programs that were to receive Smith-Hughes dollars. Albert Heusch became state supervisor of Trade and Industrial (T&I) education; W. F. Stewart, supervisor of vocational agriculture, and Maude Adams, supervisor of home economics. In addition to their supervisory responsibilities, Stewart and Adams also served as teacher trainers at The Ohio State University for their respective program areas.

During the first full year under Smith-Hughes, Ohio received approximately $2.5 million in federal vocational education aid. Nineteen vocational agriculture programs were initiated in public schools throughout the state. By 1920, 33 Ohio cities were engaged in providing evening trade or industrial schools. Two cities, Cincinnati and Toledo, offered all-day trade or industrial education programs.

When the United States entered World War I, vocational education, particularly industrial education, took on the added responsibility of a war emergency training program. The State Board for Vocational Education administered military training programs for war production workers. It also provided valuable assistance and re-training to disabled service men, enabling them to return to civilian life as productive, self-sustaining citizens.

Following the passage of the *Smith-Hughes Act*, four other federal vocational education laws were enacted that affected Ohio's vocational education program. Those laws were:

- The *George Reed Act of 1929*. It increased funding for agriculture and home economics.

- The *George-Ellzey Act of 1932*. It authorized additional funds to be shared equally among agriculture, home economics, and T&I education.

- The *George-Deen Act of 1936*. It authorized $12 million annually for 10 years to be shared equally among three program areas, changed the state/local matching provisions, and allotted annually $1 million for vocational teacher training, $1.2 million for distributive education, and another $350,000 for the U.S. Office of Education.

- The *George-Barden Act of 1946*. It renewed authorization and provided significant increases in funding for agriculture, home economics, and T&I education, $2.5 million annually for distributive education, and another $350,000 annually for the U.S. Office of Education.

During the period of time between the passage of the *Smith-Hughes Act* and World War II, the Ohio Vocational Association was founded. The organization grew out of the Ohio Society for the Promotion of Industrial Education formed in 1910 under the leadership of William T. Magruder, chairman of mechanical engineering at The Ohio State University.

In 1922, the Ohio Vocational Association held its first meeting for vocational agriculture, home economics, and T&I education teachers. Clare Sharkey, a T&I educator from Dayton presided over the meeting. In 1923, the Association elected Dean Alfred Vivian, a member of the first State Board of Vocational Education, as its first president, and Elbert Heusch, state supervisor for T&I education, as secretary.

In 1925, the Ohio Vocational Association became an affiliate of the American Vocational Association. Following passage of the *George-Deen Act* in 1936, distributive education was also recognized as a major vocational education program in Ohio. Marguerite Loos was appointed to be the first state supervisor for distributive education in 1938.

2

Vocational Education and Veterans' Training

✦

1940-1945

In the fall of 1942, the American Vocational Association (AVA), the national professional organization of vocational teachers and administrators, held its annual convention in Toledo, Ohio. The selection of Ohio was motivated by the construction in the late 1930s of Macomber Vocational High School (VHS) for boys and adults in Toledo. Macomber was named after industrialist Irving E. Macomber, who promoted the development of vocational education in the early part of the century. At the same time, the Timken Foundation (of the Timken Roller Bearing Company) built the Timken VHS in Canton, and the Whitney Vocational High School for girls was built in Toledo.

Macomber, Timken and Whitney were the most modern vocational facilities in the state and, perhaps, in the nation. All three schools had strong support of the communities and industries located in the two cities. They served not only high school youth but also adults who needed training to meet new challenges in their jobs, or new skills to secure and retain a job.

During the 1940s and early 1950s, Akron, Dayton, Cleveland and Cincinnati also built vocational high schools. All these schools maintained close relations with business and labor leaders. For many years, in its promotion announcements, the Timken Company identified the persons who had graduated from Timken VHS. The majority of the vocational high schools also developed good relations with organized labor through registered apprenticeship programs.

At this same time, there were separate vocational high schools for young women in Cincinnati, Toledo and Cleveland. Whitney VHS for Girls in Toledo was built at the same time as Macomber. The schools in Cincinnati and Cleveland were housed in older buildings. All three schools were models of outstanding vocational education in teaching the skills required for entrance into an occupation and in the development of social attitudes, modes of dress and work habits preferred in prospective employees. The leaders in these schools were Ruth S. Lape in Cincinnati, Ethel Wooden in Toledo Whitney, and Jane Addams-Eva Wingert in Cleveland.

The vocational directors in the major cities were very influential in maintaining the status of vocational education as well as the status of the state organization for vocational teachers and administrators (the Ohio Vocational Association). And it was only in the major cities that directors, principals and supervisors were employed specifically for vocational education. Among the leaders during this period were Horace Jellison, Akron; G. F. Malik, Canton; John Fintz, Cleveland; Clare Sharkey, Dayton; Carl Cotter and Frederick Dannenfelser, Toledo, and John Arundel, Cincinnati. State supervisors in vocational education in the early 1940s included Ralph Howard, Agriculture; Enid Lund, Home Economics; E. L. Heusch, T&I, and Marguerite Loos, Distributive Education.

In 1943, there were 76,301 youths and adults enrolled in vocational education in Ohio. Enrollments by program area included:

Program	High School	Adult	Apprenticeship	Total
Agriculture	10,523	5,170	NA	15,693
Business & Office	NA	NA	NA	NA
Distributive	1,140	3,666	NA	4,806
Home Economics	19,611	6,033	NA	25,644
Trade & Industrial	6,511	17,143	6,504	30,158
Totals	37,785	32,012	6,504	76,301

WAR PRODUCTION TRAINING

When the United States had entered World War I, a shortage of skilled workers had first prompted the federal government to recognize a need for vocational education. As the nation entered World War II, it was just recovering from the Great Depression and again faced a shortage of skilled workers. Millions of young men went into the Armed Forces, instantly depleting the work force. Millions of women, symbolized by "Rosie the Riveter," entered the labor force in jobs that had always been considered "men's work".

Congress passed 10 acts from 1940 to 1946 to utilize vocational education facilities across the nation to train workers for the war production industries. The federal government funded everything, including state leadership and supervision, local administrative costs, and instructional equipment and supply costs. Vocational education's successful preparation of people for the war effort established it as an important component of the country's national defense. In addition to existing training programs, two new ones emerged—Out of School Youth for National Defense (OSYND) and Vocational Education for National Defense (VEND). In Ohio, the governor assigned responsibility for these programs to the Vocational Education Services of the State Department of Education.

Ohio prepared its first *War Production Plan* in 1940. At that time, there was no overall coordination of Ohio's vocational education services. Initially, Elbert L. Heusch, T&I Education Director, was assigned the responsibility of interim Director of Vocational Education for National Defense. His staff of 11 included a general supervisor, three field assistants, two stenographers, an accountant, and four office assistants.

As the *War Production Training* program expanded, the State Board for Vocational Education appointed a full-time director, Dr. Joseph Strobel. Strobel had been a teacher of T&I education programs in Cleveland. Pursuant to his appointment as state director, Strobel was given a staff of nine, including supervisors of finance, operations, and equipment, and six part-time field supervisors. The state changed the six part-time field-supervisory positions to five full-time positions in 1942.

The state's local vocational education facilities were quickly renovated to provide training in occupations that were experiencing a shortage of skilled workers essential to the war production training initiative. The training programs operated in most T&I vocational centers, and even in some local schools that did not have T&I education. In some cases, the nature of the needed training required the federal government to purchase equipment. Lima City Schools received an entire complement of equipment to train machine-tool workers for the Lima Tank Plant.

Many vocational facilities across the state operated war production training programs until midnight on a daily basis, and in several major cities, programs operated 24 hours a day. The relatively new vocational high schools in Toledo and Canton were inundated with requests for training. The older facilities in Cleveland, Akron, Dayton, and Cincinnati were also used to capacity. While Columbus did not have a vocational building, Central High School had extensive industrial shops that were used for OSYND and VEND classes.

Teachers most frequently came from the day-school vocational programs, but the instructional load and extended hours soon made it necessary that schools hire training instructors from industry. In a number of cases, classes operated around the clock and all year long. Trained people were essential for the United States to become the arsenal of democracy. The number of workers actually trained through this war production era is not known because historical records are unavailable.

Food production was also extremely important in support of the war effort. Strobel assigned L. B. Fidler and Paul Pulse to direct the Farm War Production Training Program. Vocational agriculture programs and their instructors sponsored training on farms across the state.

Byrl Shoemaker, later to become state director of the Division of Vocational Education, recalled his own experience:

> *I directed and taught both OSYND and VEND in a small school system outside Columbus. There was a new Curtis Wright airplane plant nearby. Using the industrial arts facilities for an OSYND program, I provided adult students with skills in drafting, basic math, sheet metal layout and oxy-acetylene and electric-arc welding.*
>
> *Classes started at 4 p.m., with one class running from 4 to 8 p.m. and another from 7 to 11 p.m. Since our facilities were limited, there were only about 12 students in each class. The classroom instruction was taught in the 7 to 8 p.m. period to the total group. I taught both the day classes and the adult classes. The students received materials and instruction free of charge. I was paid $2.50 per hour, the superintendent received a small stipend to manage the program, and the school received an allowance to cover the operation's costs. Students were very faithful in their attendance. There were jobs for them upon graduation.*
>
> *As the Curtis Wright plant went into operation, sheet metal layout and light metal welding skills were in demand. Then, there was a need for the more highly skilled oxy-acetylene welders. I asked Dr. Strobel for approval to start a VEND program. We set up a separate room with 12 welding stations. Federal funds paid for all of the equipment, materials and supplies. A supervisor and one of his assis-*

tants from Curtis Wright taught two classes each night for four hours. A number of the enrollees were women. They came straight from managing a household. Some stayed, and some dropped out. Persons who completed the 10-week OSYND program went on into the VEND program. Curtis Wright hired the graduates almost immediately.

A representative of the Columbus Bolt Works testified to the success of the war production training programs:

We find those workers that have attended vocational training schools prior to their induction into defense jobs have an understanding of the work to be done, of the machines and their capabilities, of the safety hazards involved, and through this training have a general understanding of what they might expect when they accept a job in a defense plant. With this background, these trainees adapt themselves readily to new surroundings, save considerable time in adjusting themselves to new jobs to be done, and are better satisfied with the work they are doing because they have had the opportunity to decide prior to their induction into industry whether or not they are going to like this kind of work.

The final *War Production Training Act* (PL 457) was passed in 1945. Each state was required to audit all local accounts, inventory purchased equipment, and make any necessary equipment transfers. The program was to be closed down by July 1, 1945.

To operate the war training programs, Ohio received federal funds amounting to $12,981,389.56. A total of 437,846 students were enrolled in war production classes. In 1942, the peak year for pre-employment and supplementary training, Columbus alone enrolled more than 3,500 students and spent $88,500. The service rendered by vocational education from 1940 to 1945 is one of the many bright spots in the history of vocational education.

VETERANS' TRAINING

Customarily, at the conclusion of major wars, the U.S. government rewarded veterans with mustering-out pay or land grants, and provided for the financial well-being of the disabled veterans and their dependents. World War II was different. The young people, mostly men, who served their country went to war at the end of the Great Depression. In 1945-46 they were thrust back into an economy that was short of everything, including the skills and knowledge needed to secure the peace. They had the skills of war but not the skills for this new industrial age.

Over 15,440,000 veterans yearned for a future of prosperity, not poverty and more sacrifice.

The nation responded wisely and expediently. In 1944, the *Servicemen's Readjustment Act* (PL 78-346), commonly referred to as the G I Bill, passed the House of Representatives by one vote and was signed into law by President Franklin D. Roosevelt. Endorsed by the American Legion, the law required returning veterans to have served 90 days on or after 1940, and to have had an honorable discharge, in order to be eligible for benefits. The law provided several types of benefits, including:

- education stipends that included one year of training, plus a period equal to the length of service, to a maximum of 48 months;

- payments of up to $500 per year to an educational institution for tuition, books, fees, and other costs; and

- a subsistence allowance, initially $65 per month for a single veteran.

The initial G I Bill ran from 1944 to 1956. Among the 15.4 million veterans, 7.8 million received training under the G I Bill. Of these, 2.23 million received a college education; 3.48 million went to vocational schools; 1.4 million received on-the-job training, and 690,000 received farm training.

The G I Bill required a State Approval Agency (SAA) in every state. In Ohio, the Division of Vocational Education, under Strobel's direction was chosen to house its SAA. The SAA provided a monthly list of approved schools and on-the-job training sites. The Veterans Administration paid the salaries and travel for SAA staff persons in the Division of Vocational Education.

Strobel designed a system to evaluate and approve schools that wanted to provide training to veterans. Program standards were developed and adopted, and staff was hired to make site visits to schools to determine if the sites could meet the standards.

Identifying colleges and universities for approval was relatively easy, as was the approval of public education and public vocational education programs. But sensing a bonanza, entrepreneurs came out of the woodwork to establish new private schools. A number of established private schools presented few, if any problems, as did well-planned new schools. However, there were requests from "schools" set up haphazardly in garages and vacant buildings that had inadequate equipment, limited programs of instruction, and unsafe facilities. At the height of veterans training in Ohio, in 1946-47, the Veterans Training Service employed

50 people—the largest single number of employees for any program in the Division.

The SAA field staff was located in local public schools. Neither the state nor the local schools were reimbursed for space or support services, but the commitment to the veterans encouraged both to make in-kind contributions. Not a single school system refused to provide assistance. Monthly, the field staff would report to the state office on the results of their reviews. The state staff would send the field staff the names of the schools they were to visit.

Federal funding limited visits to only the on-the-job training program sites, but Ohio and other states used the funds to visit and approve other schools as well. On-the-job training programs required a commitment by employers to provide training at the place of employment. While learning a job, the veteran was paid a lower wage to compensate for the initial lack of productivity.

The veterans training program also served veterans who wanted to return to the farm or to begin farming. North Fairfield and Lisbon had the first on-the-farm programs. Programs expanded rapidly to 650 under the direction of Fidler, J. H. Lintner, and Floyd Ruble.

It should be noted that the majority of veterans opted for training other than college. Training by public and private vocational education, and on-the-job training by business and industry served the educational needs of 5.57 million veterans—a far greater number than the 2.23 million who participated in college programs. The former group made a far greater contribution to the economy than is generally acknowledged.

Over its 12-year life, the federal government invested $14.5 million in the G I Bill. Subsequent federal legislation provided similar educational benefits to veterans of the Korean War and the Vietnam War, among others. The Korean War bill (1952) covered 5.5 million veterans. Of that total, 2.4 million veterans took advantage of the G I Bill; 1.2 million received college training, 860,000 attended other vocational schools, 223,000 engaged in on-the-job training, and 95,000 participated in the on-farm training program.

The post-Korean War and the Vietnam War Bill covered the period 1966 to 1989. During that time, 1.4 million post-Korean War veterans, six million Vietnam veterans, and 751,000 other service members received training. Existing veterans' education legislation covered not only war veterans, but men and women who had served during peacetime. This legislation was known as the *Montgomery Bill*. In addition to having served in the military, beneficiaries of the *Montgomery Bill* had to have contributed a portion of their military pay towards the benefits derived.

In total, from 1944 to 1993, the federal government had invested $69.8 billion in veterans' education, with $61.7 billion directed toward education and training, $4.5 billion for vocational rehabilitation, and $3.6 billion for dependent education assistance. Currently, there is still a Veterans Education Service in the Ohio Department of Education's Office of Career-Technical and Adult Education.

Vocational education programs in Ohio and throughout the country have contributed massively to this nation's military efforts in addition to training veterans to turn swords into plowshares.

3

Need for Change

✦

1945-1956

World War II ended in 1945. The vocational education programs in Ohio and other states had successfully met the challenge of training the workers who provided the armament and food for the allied team. But now vocational education faced new challenges; training and educating returning veterans, and continuing and expanding programs of vocational education for other youth and adults.

The State Board for Vocational Education decided that it needed a leader to mold the individual service programs in vocational education into a coordinated unit. The Board appointed Strobel, who had done an excellent job of directing War Production Training, as director of vocational education in the State Department of Education.

On only one previous occasion had there been a director of vocational education. In 1920, C.H. Brady was appointed to that position, but Vernon Riegle, then state superintendent of public instruction, decided that having a director was not effective and did not re-appoint Brady.

In 1945, the vocational education program services and their respective supervisors included: agriculture, Ralph Howard; home economics, Enid Lund; distributive education, Marguerite Loos, and T&I education, E. L. Heusch. Heusch, who had lost a son in the war, had said he would retire as soon as the war was over. He took retirement the day after the peace treaty was signed with Japan. Strobel selected Robert Reese as trade and industry supervisor. Reese had been director of war production training in Indiana, but prior to his tenure in Indiana, he had grown up and taught in Ohio.

With the advent of the 1917 *Smith-Hughes Vocational Education Act*, agricultural and home economics programs flourished in small cities and rural areas. The agricultural programs were solely production agriculture oriented. Home economics dealt largely with the skills and the responsibilities of homemaking in the more rural areas.

T&I education programs were located in the larger cities where most of the construction, maintenance, service, and manufacturing jobs were located. The T&I programs were diverse and required larger student populations and greater financial investments in equipment than was the case for either agriculture or home economics.

It was already obvious that many farm youths would need to move to the cities to earn a living. But the curriculum in the small schools did not provide the skills and knowledge needed for skilled work in industry. There was also a growing concern for "school dropouts" and for those students who did not plan to go to college. In 1945 about 45% of the students who started the ninth grade graduated from high school. The basic curriculum in most schools offered either a college preparatory option or a general education course of study. Since many of the jobs in business and industry were of a repetitive production line nature, there had been little concern for those who dropped out or took the general education curriculum because they could always get a job "on the line."

Although business and office education had not yet been identified as a vocational offering, there were a number of cooperative business programs that had been approved by the State Department of Education. Since there were no in-school skill training programs for business occupations, students took general business classes and the required academic courses for half the school day. During the other half day, business students were placed in stenographic or clerical positions in the business community. The general business teacher placed the students on the job and visited them on a regular basis to evaluate their work performance.

In 1946, Congress enacted a supplemental authorization, the *George-Barden Act* (PL 79-586). That legislative enactment was an extension of the *George-Deen Act*, which had increased funding for existing vocational programs including agriculture, home economics, T&I education, and distributive education. *George-Barden* delegated more authority to state and local entities as to how federal money could be spent. That started a trend that has continued through all succeeding federal vocational education legislation.

George-Barden's provisions included:

- Ten million dollars for agricultural education, allocated on the basis of the farm population in each state;

- Support for two vocational youth organizations—Future Farmers of America and New Farmers of America;

- Eight million dollars for home economics, allocated on the basis of the rural population in each state;

- Eight million dollars for T&I education, allocated on the basis of the non-farm population in each state;

- Funds for marketing occupations to support part-time (cooperative education) and evening courses for employed workers; and

- Authorization for up to 10% of the allocated funds to purchase equipment needed in vocational education programs.

The Act did not authorize any federal funds for job preparatory programs in other fields.

Overall, George-Barden increased annual appropriations from $14 million to $29 million. It also added areas that could receive funds, including vocational education for the fishery trades and for the Office of Vocational Education in Washington, DC.

Guidance was one of the areas of educational services that benefited from the *George-Barden Act*. Strobel decided guidance services were important to youth as they made choices of educational programs, especially vocational education choices. The Division of Vocational Education hired John Odgers to direct guidance efforts across the state. In the early 1960s, additional funds from other federal programs provided financial assistance to states to expand guidance programs.

Reese and Lawrence Borosage began a limited number of T&I education programs in many medium-sized cities, including Lima, Findlay, Fostoria, Lorain, Ashtabula, and Portsmouth. Believing that program growth depended on local leadership, Reese provided financial assistance to those cities to employ supervisors of T&I education. Reese required the supervisors to start programs for adults who needed technical knowledge or new/additional job related skills. The adult programs became very popular and in themselves justified the investment in local leadership.

The T&I supervisors' group grew to about 40. Together, with the T&I education leaders from the major cities, the group met annually for two to three weeks of training in principles of program operations and innovative practices. That cadre of enthusiastic leaders became a major force for growth and change in vocational education in Ohio.

As a mean of reaching out to even smaller cities, a program was developed for "diversified occupations" (D.O.). Students spent the morning studying materials related to their chosen occupations. Diversified occupation teachers were called coordinators. They had responsibility for placing students with employers for the second half of the school day. The D.O. program proved very popular. By the middle 1950s, there were approximately 45 such programs in the state.

During Strobel's tenure, state funding for vocational education remained relatively static and limited. He managed the division well, motivated staff and was an excellent speaker. He did not, however, increase funding. That limitation seriously hampered program growth. When Strobel accepted a professorship at The Ohio State University in 1952 to guide the vocational teacher education program, Ralph Howard, supervisor of vocational agriculture, became director.

Howard was a different type of leader. He was a quiet man with a sound philosophy of vocational education, great integrity and political savvy, but he did not possess Strobel's charisma or his speaking ability. In many small communities, the vocational agriculture teachers had longer tenures and had developed better contacts with community leadership than their respective local superintendents. Utilizing this network of agricultural teachers, Howard gradually increased state funding for vocational education that stimulated program growth.

In 1953 the Ohio legislature authorized a vote on a constitutional amendment to create a State Board of Education. The amendment passed. The General Assembly then established a 23-member State Board of Education with one member to be elected from each of Ohio's congressional districts. Electing a large board by congressional districts was more an issue of politics than philosophy of government. Republicans controlled the General Assembly, but Governor Frank Lausche was a Democrat. The Republican legislative majority was not about to let a Democratic governor appoint the members of the new Board of Education. Subsequently, the elected State Board of Education played a key role in the massive changes and growth of vocational education programs throughout the state.

At about the same time that the elected state board was seated, the General Assembly also appointed an education study commission, led by Rep. William L. Manahan of Defiance. In 1955 the Manahan Commission crafted 106 recommendations. Eleven of the commission recommendations related to how public education should be organized at the state level. Other recommendations related to educational funding.

At one commission hearing, when educational funding patterns were being discussed, T & I assistant supervisor, Byrl Shoemaker, made a plea for vocational education programs to be funded for an additional unit. The Commission listened courteously, but did not vote to allocate such a unit. Shortly thereafter, Manahan left the hearing room briefly. Amanda Thomas, lobbyist for the Retail Merchants Association, approached Manahan when he was out of the room. She made a strong plea for the additional vocational unit funding. Manahan returned to the meeting and stated that vocational education programs would be funded for an additional unit. The Retail Merchants Association's belief in the value of vocational education contributed significantly to vocational education's future. A funding mechanism was now in place that encouraged program growth and expansion throughout the state.

Although guidance services had been added to the Division of Vocational Education, the broad area of business and office education was still not a part of the division framework. The Ohio Business Teachers Association lobbied for its inclusion in the vocational education family. In 1955, it found a willing advocate in Howard. That year the business teachers' organization of the Ohio Education Association invited him to speak at its regional meeting in southern Ohio. Encouraged by the efforts of the business education teachers, Howard requested funds for vocational business and office education. The funding request, however, was not included in the General Assembly's 1955-56 state biennium budget.

Led by the Division's T&I Education service, 25 community surveys were conducted in 1955-57 to identify areas of vocational education important to the local communities' employment patterns. Division representatives met with persons appointed by local school superintendents to identify major employment opportunities. At dinner meetings sponsored by local school systems the organization and operation of vocational education were explained.

Employers were asked to complete questionnaires on employee needs and projections in selected occupations. Information was gathered on employer interest in vocational education programs. Employers were also asked whether they would participate in cooperative education programs should in-school vocational education programs not be available. Employers who could not attend the dinner meetings received visits the following day by Division of Vocational Education staff members and local school representatives. The Division reported the survey results to the respective school districts.

In every city surveyed, employers indicated keen interest in vocational education. Even though the interest was obvious, the limited student population in most school districts and the limited tax base for financial support did not permit the initiation of new vocational education program offerings. However, in some communities, cooperative education programs were initiated in areas such as distributive education and diversified occupations. Students enrolled in cooperative vocational education programs attended school for half of the day to obtain the necessary academic and vocational theory instruction, and then worked in an actual job for pay for the remainder of the school day to learn the necessary employment-related skills.

The survey results and the public meetings further motivated the leadership in T&I education to find ways to meet the discerned needs for more vocational education, especially in trades and industry. Reese hosted a vocational educator from New York who had initiated a program in which seven school districts had each added one or two vocational areas to their curriculum. Home school buses traveled to all seven districts to transport students enrolled in specific vocational education offerings.

The New York guest spent three days with the T&I staff, explaining all aspects of the vocational programs of choice. On the third day, he asked, *Do you understand how it operates?* The response from the group was a resounding, *Yes!* The New Yorker responded wryly, *Don't do it. The participating students attend neighboring bastions of competition and they are never comfortable.* So much for what looked like a real possibility for change. The question remained: How does Ohio provide adequate programs of vocational education accessible to all students in a state that has 800 school districts?

In 1956, Reese had completed his PhD studies and was appointed to a professorship in vocational education at The Ohio State University. Howard appointed Byrl Shoemaker as supervisor of T&I education. Shoemaker shared Reese's passion to provide a broad program of vocational T&I education to all youth.

Shoemaker visited the Bucks County Area Vocational School in Pennsylvania. Bucks County bussed students from a number of school districts to a central point for vocational training. Students were bussed in for a half-day program. They then returned to their home schools for their academic classes.

Impressed with the Bucks County operation, Shoemaker wondered how the students received the related math or science associated with their respective occupational areas. Most programs in the school required applied mathematics and science, but dealt only with the T&I occupations. He received permission to have students in two of the classes write down the subjects they were taking at their home schools. A review of that information indicated students <u>were not</u> taking academic math and science courses at their home schools, even though the subjects were available to them—and there was no time at the vocational school to teach applied math and science.

From this experience, Shoemaker decided that:

1. An area vocational school concept would bring together the number of students and the tax base needed to support a comprehensive vocational education program.

2. Students needed to have the related mathematics and science taught at the area vocational school. That would assure that such instruction was available and there would be an economy of class size to warrant the instruction.

3. An area vocational school should not be limited to T&I education, but should include offerings in agriculture, business, and distributive occupations.

The concept of an area vocational school seemed sound, but the idea was foreign to vocational educators in Ohio, except in the seven major cities, Those districts had established vocational high schools to draw students from throughout the city. Thus, they could provide comprehensive programming, matching the interests of students with the needs of employers. The vocational high schools also provided facilities and classroom space for the instruction of apprentices engaged in skill training in the construction and manufacturing industries. Additionally, these vocational high schools offered classes to upgrade adult workers' skills and technical knowledge.

By 1956, vocational education enrollment in Ohio had increased significantly.

Enrollments in Vocational Education in Ohio (1956)

Program	All-Day & Day Unit	Evening	Part-time	Extension	Cooperative	Total
Agriculture	11,432	5,615	2,099	--	--	19,146
Distributive Occupations		5,527	1,689	825	864	8,905
Home Economics	15,428	10,827	2,219	--	--	28,474
Trades & Industry	4,983	22,925	9,469	8,226	1,101	46,704
Total	31,843	44,894	15,476	9,051	1,965	103,229

In that year, Congress passed the *George-Barden Amendments* (PL84-911). The act had a limited purpose. It added funds for practical nursing ($5 million) and fishery occupations ($375,000) to a list of approved programs of instruction.

But the act also included an important concept; a five-year authorization to use federal funds in the construction of area vocational schools. This marked the first time that federal funds could be used to build area vocational schools.

4

Winds of Change

✦

1957-1962

As the 1950s progressed, there were increasingly significant efforts to consolidate Ohio school districts to improve and expand educational offerings. In a number of rural schools, the student bodies were too small to offer multiple science and mathematics courses in the same year.

A review of national employment patterns revealed that approximately 16% of the jobs in the economy required a college degree. Employment was divided into the following major sectors:

Employment Sector	Percent of Workers
Agriculture	9.0
Retail and Wholesale	14.7
Business	14.4
T&I	42.2
Professional	7.6
Other	12.1

These data indicated that the large majority of youth graduating from high school entered employment in occupations that did not require a college degree. Also, data clearly indicated the number of available unskilled occupations was shrinking. The price of admission to the new age was, at the minimum, a high school education as well as the skills and knowledge required for an occupation in the post-industrial age.

It was exceedingly clear that a comprehensive menu of vocational education could not be provided in any school with limited enrollment. Based upon student interests and employment opportunities, adjusted for local and state employment patterns, a comprehensive menu of vocational education, at minimum, was defined to include:

- Two agricultural education programs
- Three business and office education programs
- One distributive education program
- Six T&I education programs

Since the large majority of available jobs would not require a college education, the problem of expanding opportunities for youths to prepare for employment during their last two years of high school became a major focus of the State Division of Vocational Education. Shoemaker, in his new role as supervisor of T&I education, encouraged his staff to look for a county or group of school districts that had the means and interest to pilot an area school concept.

Phillip Anderson, T&I area supervisor in southern Ohio, found one of the school buildings in Pike County was vacant as a result of the county's shrinking public school enrollment. In addition, Pike County had some residual funds from the federal government's recent construction of a nearby uranium enrichment plant. These surplus funds could be used for program innovation.

J.E. Way was the Pike County superintendent of schools. His son Chester Way was assistant superintendent of schools. "Chet" Way became interested in the possibility of an area vocational school to serve all of the public school districts in Pike County. He made the vacant building available and provided the funds to equip and operate an area vocational school.

Initially, three programs were selected. Much of the equipment was obtained from government surplus. The programs began in the fall of 1957. The organization and operation of the area vocational school were governed by the following principles and practices:

- All of the teachers were occupationally competent.
- Enrollment was limited to 11th grade male students.
- Students were transported to the area vocational school site by their home school districts. Students would travel to their respective home schools via regular school bus routes. A single bus would then transport the vocational students to the area school site.

- Conversely, buses would pick up the students 30 minutes before the end of their respective home school day to return to their home schools to be transported home via the regular school bus routes. To optimize instructional time, there were no study halls at the area school site.

- Students at the area vocational school had three hours of hands-on experience in their chosen occupation; one and one-half hours of technically related instruction, including the related mathematics and science, and 11th grade English, a state requirement for high school graduation.

- Vocational students would participate in common vocational classes and laboratories during the day and compete against each on their home high school athletic teams after school.

After the area vocational school's first year of operation, local school administrators changed their minds regarding female participation at the area vocational school. Cosmetology was added to the vocational education offerings.

The area vocational school concept worked better than originally anticipated. The curriculum offerings in each of the six school districts were expanded by the number of vocational offerings at the center. In the first three years of operation there was one altercation, and that was between two boys from the same district. The local educational leadership and the state vocational staff judged the pilot effort a success.

State vocational education leaders believed all Ohio youths should have access to a comprehensive program of vocational education while in high school. The staff never had any idea of forcing youths into vocational programs, but it became obvious school consolidation was never going to bring about large enough high school units to make opportunities in vocational education available to all youth in Ohio. High school students should have the opportunity, state vocational education leaders believed, to enroll in programs of choice. That became the goal of the staff of the Division of Vocational Education.

SPUTNIK AND TECHNICAL EDUCATION

The Soviet Union's 1957 launch of Sputnik raised a great concern in the United States about its ability to compete with Soviet technology. The accusing finger pointed at public education. This nation's educational system was perceived to be a failure. There were huge manpower shortages in electronics, aerospace engineering, mathematics, foreign languages, and other highly technical occupations.

Congress quickly passed the *National Defense Education Act of 1958* (NDEA) (PL85-864). NDEA was the first legislation to emphasize mathematics, science, foreign languages, and technical knowledge and skills. However, the law focused on post-secondary and adult populations rather than the high school youth.

But Titles VIII and IX encouraged the area school concept and provided funds to establish and maintain vocational schools to serve individuals, geographic regions, and occupations that were not being adequately accommodated by existing vocational education systems. Congress' intent was to encourage programs that emphasized a combination of applied skills and technical knowledge, including mathematics, science, and related technology. The goal was to produce technician aides to engineers and scientists. Assistant Secretary of Education Jack Walsh, leader of T&I Education in the U.S. Office of Education, picked up on the intent of Congress. He encouraged the state leadership in T&I education to establish technical education programs at the post-secondary educational level.

In late 1958, Shoemaker visited the Erie County New York Technical Institute to observe programs preparing post-secondary students for this new level of occupations, a level between the skilled trades and engineering professionals. Enthused by what he saw, he began developing an Ohio program. In 1959, with support from industry, a technical institute bill was introduced into the Ohio legislature. It authorized the Division of Vocational Education to initiate two-year, post-high school technical institutes to train students to work at the paraprofessional level. The General Assembly passed the bill, but the presidents of Miami University at Oxford, The Ohio State University and Ohio University at Athens persuaded Governor Michael V. DiSalle to veto it.

However, that was not the end of the story. With the support of a major local industry that needed technicians to support its engineers, Kenneth Herbert, T&I education supervisor at Barberton City Schools, began an experimental program in mechanical and chemical technologies in 1959. The program proved to be quite successful. Yet in 1965, when Akron University became a public state university, the Barberton program was phased out.

Subsequently, since federal NDEA funds had been made available to the state of Ohio, Shoemaker decided to initiate the establishment of two-year, post-high school technical institutes without the benefit of legislative authorization. He organized a state technical advisory committee to design the curriculum. Two technical institutes were begun in 1960, one in Lorain, the other in Springfield.

Under the leadership of Dr. Max Lerner, T&I education supervisor in the Lorain Public Schools, a surplus elementary school building was used to house the technical institute. Faculty members were recruited from among professional engineers. Jesse Fulton, general office manager at Addressograph-Multigraph Company, chaired the local advisory committee. The committee recommended a curriculum requiring 2,500 faculty-student contact hours in class, shop, and laboratory over the two-year curriculum. Instruction was offered in three engineering technology programs. A great effort was needed to motivate high school graduates to enroll in programs that were entirely new in Ohio.

The other technical institute program started in Springfield High School in the late afternoon and evening under the direction of Richard Brinkman. Brinkman had been the assistant county superintendent of education and was developing an area vocational school for Clark County. The programs were also engineering-related and met the standards established by the state advisory committee.

While the technical institutes did not have the support of the top administrators at The Ohio State University, Dean Harold A. Boles of the OSU engineering department told Shoemaker he would assist in program development—provided that the commitment was to prepare engineering technicians and not ill-equipped engineers. Boles indicated that each engineer would need the support of about four technicians to function effectively. He said the increased knowledge and skills required of engineers no longer permitted them to do technician-level work as they had in earlier years.

While initial technical institute efforts centered on preparing engineering technicians, the Division of Vocational Education worked to establish paraprofessional programs in all fields in which the professions would accept a paraprofessional and would assist in designing the curriculum. The post-high school technical institute movement in Ohio was responsible for developing programs in agriculture, business, distribution, and home economics in addition to the engineering occupations related to T&I education.

As the joint vocational school movement progressed in Ohio, a number of separate technical institute and joint vocational school facilities were built on shared campuses. This was particularly true, in southern Ohio where the *Appalachian Regional Development Act* provided funds to build and equip joint vocational schools and technical institute centers at no, or significantly reduced, additional burden to the local real estate tax base. Such federal assistance was possible because the funds appropriated under ARDA could be used to provide financial assistance to education if such assistance would promote economic development in the region. As joint vocational districts and facilities were established in Appalachian Ohio, ARDA funds were allocated to several of the new joint vocational districts to offset construction and educational equipment costs.

During one of Shoemaker's speaking forays to business leaders in southern Ohio, a businessman asked him, *Could a technical institute program be developed for the ceramic industry?* Shoemaker responded, *I'm not sure, but I will find out.* The next day he contacted the ceramic engineering department at The Ohio State University and received an enthusiastic positive response. That was the beginning of the ceramic technology program at the Hocking Valley Technical Institute.

From 1960 to 1968 the Division of Vocational Education provided leadership to establish 14 technical education institutes. Subsequently, all but three became technical or community colleges. Hocking Valley Technical College is the only one of the original technical institutes to retain the "technical" identifier as part of its name. Eleven of the initial technical institutes transitioned to community college or state college status while the Cleveland and Salem technical institutes no longer exist.

The remaining original technical institutes in Ohio included Belmont (Belmont Community College), Canton (Stark State College), Cleveland (Cuyahoga Community College), Columbus (Columbus State College), Tri County (Hocking State College), Muskingum (Zane State College), Penta County (Owens State College), Great Oaks (Southern State College), Springfield Clark (Clark State College), Vanguard (Terra Tech State College), Washington County (Washington County State College), and Willoughby (Lakewood Community College).

As the number of technical institutes grew, Governor Rhodes sponsored technical education conferences around the state under the leadership of the Division of Vocational Education. The first Governor's Conference on Technical Education was held in Columbus to inform business and industry leaders and educators about technical education. The conference also reviewed curriculum-development processes and methods for preparing paraprofessionals.

In April 1967, the second conference took place in Cleveland. It focused on defining technical education and reviewing the progress of post-high school technical education in Ohio. Recommendations for expanding technical education were also an outgrowth of the Cleveland conference.

Using the theme *Jobs and Progress*, the third conference was held in Cincinnati in 1969. It was an invitational symposium on the implications of manpower needs for vocational/technical education. It addressed how government, business, industry, agriculture, civic/social organizations, and education could best work together to prepare people for jobs and create jobs for people. The conference attracted 600 attendees.

In 1967, the Ohio General Assembly created the State Board of Regents for public colleges and universities. Governor Rhodes selected John Millet, president of Miami University, as the first chancellor. Shoemaker recalls that initially Millet said technical education would remain within the Division of Vocational Education. But soon he decided he wanted the Board of Regents to oversee technical education. According to Shoemaker, Millet said, *We can give the associate degree and you can't.*

Purportedly, Governor Rhodes initially wanted to leave the responsibility for oversight of technical education with the Division of Vocational Education, but Millet convinced him to turn it over to the Regents as a higher education program. The Governor acceded to Millet's wishes, and the responsibility for administering technical education was transferred to the Board of Regents.

To discourage competition for adult vocational programs and apprenticeship-related classes, the State Board of Education and the Board of Regents drew up a memorandum of agreement (MOA). Under the agreement, the Division of Vocational Education agreed to continue to reimburse the technical institutes for programs that met Division standards for technical education, and the Board of Regents agreed not to duplicate the vocational program offerings for youth and adults provided at vocational education centers.

The MOA included the following principles governing the expansion of educational opportunities for vocational and technical education:

1. Determination concerning the need for, and organization of, vocational education shall be made by the Ohio State Board of Education and by the individual school districts.

2. Determinations concerning the need for, and organization of, technical education shall be made by the individual institutions of higher education.

3. On the basis of a legal and financial commitment to technical education, the Department of Education will cooperate with the Ohio Board of Regents in the development and support of technical education. Such assistance from the Department of Education shall be limited to those technical programs meeting the technical education standards of the department and shall not handicap the development of vocational education.

4. Where technical education will grow in several different administrative patterns, there must be no duplication of effort or taxation. Technical

education may develop in community colleges, stand-alone entities, or in conjunction with joint vocational school districts or university branch campuses.

5.   Cooperative efforts will be undertaken for the joint use of certain physical facilities and of appropriate professional staff and ancillary services in those circumstances where technical and vocational education programs have been established in close proximity of each other.

In 1969, the General Assembly, through HB 531, officially placed technical education under the Board of Regents. The funding provided by the Division of Vocational Education for technical education continued to be of value to the post-secondary centers. According to Shoemaker, technical institute administrators would cite the financial assistance from the Division of Vocational Education whenever faculty wanted to "water down" instruction to adjust instructional loads to those of four-year colleges.

AN ADEQUATE PROGRAM OF VOCATIONAL EDUCATION FOR ALL YOUTH

During the 1950s and 1960s, the establishment of comprehensive programs of vocational education was virtually impossible because Ohio had 800 school districts, most too small for any breadth of program. In addition, while students in metropolitan areas had greater choices in vocational education, such choices were limited in occupations related to agriculture and natural resources conservation. Based on the success of the Pike County area vocational school pilot initiative, the area school/vocational center concept seemed to be a viable way to overcome the limitations created by small enrollments and limited options.

At the urging of the Division of Vocational Education, the Ohio General Assembly passed an area school bill in 1959. This legislation permitted the establishment of area vocational centers as joint vocational school districts. The governor signed the bill, but the law was an enabling piece of legislation. There was no requirement that joint vocational schools be established.

In addition, the law appeared to have a serious problem. Any local, exempted village, or city school district that elected to become a member of a joint vocational school district could also opt out at a later date. Shoemaker saw this as a fatal flaw and made no attempt to organize area schools under the 1959 law.

In 1961, the General Assembly revised the law, but did not remove the option for a local school that had joined a joint vocational school district to drop out at the end of any school year. Consequently, any bonding by the joint vocational school district for construction and equipment costs could place unreasonable tax burdens on remaining participating districts should one or more districts elect to no longer participate in the joint vocational school arrangement.

Again, the Division of Vocational Education made no attempt to establish area centers. The early 1960s was a stressful period in our nation. Youth unemployment and underemployment generally were rocketing at the same time that there was a critical shortage of technicians and skilled workers. Industry had to constantly retrain workers as they were being displaced by automation and technology. These economic and employment issues hastened the need for innovative educational programs at the secondary and post-secondary education levels.

AREA REDEVELOPMENT ACT OF 1961

The federal *Area Redevelopment Act of 1961* (PL 87-27) was intended to provide retraining opportunities to individuals in economically depressed areas. A large section of southeastern Ohio was eligible for assistance. It provided funds for building area vocational schools and technical institutes.

MANPOWER TRAINING

In 1962, Congress debated a bill to create a program to train adults. At first, the legislation did not include vocational education as a resource to train adults. American Vocational Association Executive Director M.D. Mobley asked Dr. Jack Nix, Georgia's vocational education director, and Shoemaker to testify before both houses of Congress to promote the inclusion of the vocational education services.

These two were successful in urging Congress to make use of state vocational facilities. Subsequently, Congress passed the *Manpower Development and Training Act* (MDTA) (PL 87-415). The Department of Labor administered the funds at the federal level; state and local employment agencies handled them within the states.

As the MDTA was initiated, targeted business and industry benefactors found it difficult to utilize the program. They judged the qualifications of prospective employee participants to be insufficient. They argued that existing industries could not be revitalized with the type of people eligible for training under MDTA.

However, the Division of Vocational Education took advantage of the funds MDTA made available. It established a Manpower Training Center at a military air base near Youngstown. In addition to the manpower training funds, monies were provided by the state employment services agency and a Youngstown Foundation. The training center enrolled unemployed youth and young adults from inner cities across Ohio. The center was a laboratory for learning about the problems faced by young adults. In some cases, the instructors had to start at a very elementary level. Many students could not read. But there were essentially no discipline problems. The education and training costs per trainee were approximately $4,000.

Don Watson, who later became Springfield-Clark County Joint Vocational School District superintendent, directed the center. The Manpower Training Center was so successful that the U.S. Department of Labor (DOL) used it as a prototype to seek legislation to establish similar centers throughout the nation, but then DOL abruptly discontinued further funding for the Youngstown center.

Under various acts of Congress, manpower legislation continued for about ten years. The acts were always administered by DOL. However, Congress decided the investments in manpower training were not achieving the desired goals and did not enact further sustaining legislation.

5

Adequate Program for All

✦

1963-1969

In 1963, the U. S. Congress and the Ohio General Assembly each passed legislation important to vocational education. Congress passed the *Vocational Education Act of 1963*. Its funding provided Ohio additional money for starting area vocational schools. Then the General Assembly approved joint vocational school district legislation permitting school districts to irrevocably join together to provide vocational programs. Together these laws made it possible for Ohio to expand vocational education for youth and adults throughout the state.

VOCATIONAL EDUCATION ACT OF 1963

Federal manpower programs were directed at the training needs of adults. Something needed to be done for those youths who were quitting school with no employment skills. The *Vocational Education Act of 1963* (PL 88-210) sought to solve the problem of growing unemployment and underemployment among the nation's youth, as well as a critical shortage of skilled and technical workers.

The Act required that 90% of its funds be allocated on the basis of state populations. Funds could be spent for:

1. High school vocational education;

2. Vocational education for individuals who, having completed or discontinued their high school education, were available for full-time study to prepare for employment;

3. Vocational education for persons already employed but needing training or retraining to achieve employment stability or advancement;

4. Vocational education for persons with academic, socioeconomic, or other handicaps that prevented them from succeeding in the regular vocational programs. (Ten percent of the funds were to be spent on research and development of experimental programs to better serve the needs of persons with disabilities who could not succeed in regular vocational programs.);

5. Construction of area vocational programs; and

6. Ancillary services such as teacher training, vocational guidance, job placement, curriculum development, state leadership development, and other activities to insure quality in all vocational programs.

Other important provisions included:

1. A national advisory committee to advise the Commissioner of Education on training requirements;

2. Permission for states to transfer or combine training allotments to meet their individual needs;

3. A review committee, appointed in 1966, to study the progress in vocational education programs and recommend improvements, and

4. Work-study programs to allow students with financial need to become employed in order to begin or continue vocational education.

The act also broadened the definition of vocational education, defining it as *training or retraining which is given in schools or classes under public supervision and control or under contract with a state board or local education agency, and is conducted as a part of a program designed or fit individuals for gainful employment as semi-skilled or skilled workers or technicians in recognized occupations.*

In addition to these provisions, the act provided Ohio an additional $10 million to improve existing vocational education programs.

JOINT VOCATIONAL SCHOOL DISTRICT LAW

In 1963, the Ohio General Assembly decided to review joint vocational school district laws from 1959 and 1961. Proposed legislation changed the existing law to make it feasible for districts to join together in a broad vocational education program.

In the House, Republican B. A. Broughton of Geauga County assumed leadership for a new joint vocational school law. Vern Riffe, then a new minority Democratic House member from Scioto County, co-sponsored the bill. The bill passed both houses without any strong opposition, and Governor Rhodes signed it into law.

Section 3311.18 of the Ohio Revised Code, *Creation of Joint Vocational Schools*, corrected problems in the earlier joint vocational school laws. It stated:

> *Subject to the consent of the board of education of each school district whose territory is proposed to be included within a joint vocational school district, the initiating unit may create a joint vocational school district within the county or within an area comprised of two or more adjoining counties, composed of the territory of all the school districts whose boards of education have approved the formation of the joint vocational school district. The effective date of the establishment of such district shall be designated by the initiating unit. The boards of education of the school districts participating in the establishment of a joint vocational school district may participate on a proportional basis in meeting the administrative, clerical, and other expenses necessary to the establishment and operation of a joint vocational school district until funds are otherwise provided. A school district shall not lose its separate identity by reason of becoming a part of a joint vocational school district. Expenditures made by a participating school district in the establishment of a joint vocational school district for meeting the administrative, clerical and other expenses necessary to the establishment and operation of a joint vocational school district until such time as the joint vocational school district commences to receive revenues as provided by law are hereby ratified and declared to have been made, the same as if such contributions had been lawful at the time they were made.*

School districts that now entered into a jointure could no longer secede and place a financial burden on the remaining districts. But the law was still permissive. It did not require districts to take action. It simply permitted them to join together by a vote of the participating boards of education. The jointure board would be composed of representatives from participating boards. Funding for construction or remodeling, equipment and operation for the area vocational school had to be approved by the voters in the participating school districts.

The law gave the Division of Vocational Education a "hunting license," in the words of Shoemaker, then director of vocational education. The division had $10 million from the 1963 *Vocational Education Act*. The money could be allocated to ongoing programs or to improvements in areas such as teacher education.

Shoemaker decided to use it to encourage development of joint vocational districts.

The division announced it would pay half the cost of new construction or the remodeling of vocational education facilities—and half the cost of equipping joint vocational schools. However, to be eligible for the federal funds, districts had to form a joint vocational school district, and vote their share for construction, equipment and operation. This placed the voters of any new joint vocational school district in the driver's seat. Shoemaker based his plan on the notion that by giving the people something worthwhile they would approve the additional taxes.

State Superintendent of Public Instruction Dr. E. E. Holt was very supportive of vocational education. He had served as superintendent in five school districts. But he did not believe school districts would voluntarily join together. When Governor Rhodes signed the joint vocational school bill into law, recalled Shoemaker, Holt placed an arm around Shoemaker's shoulders, and said, *Work your heart out, Byrl, but there will never be a joint vocational school in Ohio.*

In the early stages of the joint vocational school movement, Ohio had 710 local, exempted village and city school districts. County superintendents believed that there were still too many school districts, but consolidations had caused many hard feelings, and had about run their course.

The multitude of districts limited what could be accomplished in vocational education. But the state Division of Vocational Education and the county superintendents were the only ones encouraging development of area vocational schools.

Gallup Poll statistics had always revealed strong public support for providing youth with the skills to earn a living, said Shoemaker. *Unlike academicians who were only concerned with college entrance requirements, the people knew the large majority of youth would enter employment without a college degree. They knew, too, that only a small percent of jobs required a college degree.*

According to Shoemaker:

> A very fortuitous occurrence provided vocational and technical education with a powerful ally in Governor Rhodes. When he became governor, Rhodes established committees across department lines to share information. State Superintendent Holt appointed me to serve on one of the committees.
>
> I was invited to present information on the Division of Vocational Education. Assistant Director of the Department of Finance Howard Collier was present and heard my presentation. Afterwards, he asked me to provide him with all available information on the organization and operation of vocational education.

Collier reviewed the information thoroughly and discussed it with Rhodes. The governor was committed to building business and industry to improve Ohio's job opportunities and its economy. He saw vocational education as a way to support his efforts.

> *Always quick to understand an area of assistance, the governor took vocational education under his wing and gave it full support,* recalled Shoemaker. *The governor's interest was not in a philosophy of education, but in a source of training for both youth and adults. He truly wanted youth to graduate with a diploma in one hand and a job in the other.*

During Rhodes' four terms as governor, he supported the development and growth of vocational and technical education, and utilized these services to expand economic development and job opportunities throughout Ohio.

Rhodes invited Shoemaker to join him when he met with industry leaders. When General Motors closed its appliance manufacturing operations in Dayton, but offered to reopen the plants to make new products, Rhodes sent Shoemaker to Dayton with instructions to give General Motors whatever support it requested to retrain the appliance workers to manufacture new products. In cooperation with the Dayton Pubic Schools, more than 2,000 workers received training. General Motors' president stated the training had provided the smoothest plant opening the company had ever experienced.

SUPPORT FROM STATE GOVERNMENT, EDUCATORS AND ORGANIZATIONS

Shoemaker believed that throughout the years of growth of vocational education support by the governor, both parties in the Ohio General Assembly, and local voters were the keys to the vocational education movement's success.

A number of superintendents, particularly county superintendents and some city superintendents also gave their support. The State Board of Education stood firm in managing major challenges. All state superintendents of public instruction supported the movement. During Holt's term as state superintendent, Shoemaker was permitted to contact the legislature to promote vocational education. Shoemaker indicated that he was extremely careful not to involve himself in any school legislation except that related to vocational education. However, when Dr.

Martin Essex became state superintendent, he directed that only one person, who reported to him, should deal with the legislature.

That was a critical time for vocational education legislation. Shoemaker felt he had to relay his ideas and concerns to legislators. He worked through local vocational education leaders.

Three joint vocational school superintendents were particularly effective. They were Eugene Kavanagh (Green County), William Ramsey (Penta County), and Richard Brinkman (Springfield-Clark). They worked with the state superintendent's legislative liaison and individual legislators. Governor Rhodes also continued to involve Shoemaker in legislation and in the promotion of business and industry growth.

Dr. Franklin B. Walter, superintendent of public instruction from 1977 to 1991, made the most important contributions. Walter gave direct support to the movement as assistant state superintendent. He traveled with division staff members as they took standards to school districts and visited JVS districts that were completing their area school organizational plans. When he became state superintendent, Walter also raised the status of the Division of Vocational and Career Education within the Department of Education by appointing Shoemaker to executive director status.

Walter advocated vocational education with the State Board of Education, and monitored the division's work to be sure it maintained thorough and accurate records.

POLICY ON USE OF FEDERAL FUNDS

In 1968 State Finance Director Howard Collier made an in-depth review of the allocations and expenditure of all federal and state funds by the Division of Vocational Education.

After this review, Collier called Shoemaker in to discuss an administrative policy that became very important to vocational education. Satisfied with the division's management of federal funds, Collier established a policy of using Ohio's federal funds for program improvement, including the area of leadership development, and not for the operation of secondary programs at the local level. This policy was, and continues to be, extremely instrumental to the division's leadership role in vocational and career education.

OHIO VOCATIONAL ASSOCIATION

The Ohio Vocational Association (OVA), the professional organization for vocational and technical education was formed in 1922. At first it restricted its membership to those working in vocational education, but by the mid-1960s anyone interested in supporting vocational education was welcome. While most members were vocational program teachers and administrators, there were, in all, seven categories of membership.

Dr. Ralph Woodin, professor of agricultural education at The Ohio State University, volunteered as OVA executive director from the late 1950s to 1965. Ohio State University vocational education professor Dr. Robert Reese then became the volunteer executive director in 1965. After retiring from Ohio State University in 1973, Reese continued as a half-time paid director until 1977. Jack Freeh succeeded Reese as the full-time director, and was followed by Alice Karen Hite in 1984, a post she held until 1999. Since Hite's 15-year tenure as executive director, the position has returned to part-time status.

OVA sponsored an annual conference for all members, and offered in-service training and support for its members. The association represented teachers and administrators at the state and national levels. OVA worked vigorously to support vocational education legislation. In cooperation with the state Division of Vocational Education, OVA organized an annual breakfast or dinner for Ohio's U.S. representatives and senators. In addition, it joined with the Ohio Association of Joint Vocational School Superintendents to sponsor annual statewide vocational education legislative seminars involving state representatives and senators.

On October 9, 1998, the Ohio Vocational Board of Directors voted to change the name of the Ohio Vocational Association to the Ohio Association for Career and Technical Education, contingent upon approval by the delegates to the annual convention of the American Vocational Association to change its name the Association for Career and Technical Education (ACTE). This occurred at the annual convention in New Orleans in December 1998. The name change was in keeping with the incorporation of the name "career and technical education" in the *Carl D. Perkins Vocational and Technical Education Act of 1998* (P.L. 105-332).

In 1998, the Ohio ACTE included eight membership categories and 12 divisions.

FORMATION OF JOINT VOCATIONAL SCHOOL DISTRICTS

Two geographic areas in Ohio were the first to take advantage of state and federal legislation in 1963 authorizing the development of joint vocational school districts. Led by William Ramsey, superintendent of Rossford Schools, 17 local school districts from the Toledo area convened local school board members in the Rossford High School auditorium. Shoemaker explained the process to create a joint vocational school (JVS) district.

Immediately after his presentation the individual districts convened meetings in the auditorium. All 17 agreed to establish the Penta County JVS District. The name reflected the participation of school districts from a five-county area.

The federal government agreed to donate a large section of a surplus warehouse facility to the new district. The donated site included a building that Shoemaker approved for remodeling to house the JVS. The Division of Vocational Education provided federal funds to cover half the cost of remodeling and equipping the building. Ramsey was named superintendent of the newly created district. Voters in the 17 local and city school districts approved local taxes to cover the other half of the renovation costs and to operate the JVS.

The JVS district also received operating funds from the state education foundation. The Division of Vocational Education supported programs to retrain adult workers and/or to upgrade their employment skills.

The Penta County JVS district then launched a post-secondary technical institute initiative that subsequently became known as Owens Community College and then Owens State College. The Penta County JVS opened in the fall of 1965. John Kurfess, father of the speaker of the State House Representative Charles Kurfess, was the first JVS district board president.

A second JVS center opened in 1965 in Lake County. Henry LaMuth, Lake County Schools superintendent, led its development. The property tax burden on homeowners of the participating local districts in this new JVS district was one of the highest in Ohio. Yet Lake County voters approved the required funds the first time the issue appeared on the ballot. The JVS, now the Auburn Career Center, has served youth and adults from its beginning.

The development of JVS centers continued, but it was necessary to convince each group of school districts regarding the merits of forming a JVS. Passing tax levies was always a problem. After one particularly difficult election day, when several JVS district levies were defeated, Shoemaker went to Governor Rhodes to seek help. The governor called a representative of the Ohio Manufacturers Association (OMA) to his office, and asked for his association's support for JVS levies. OMA's actions were never publicized, but JVS levies passed with greater and greater frequency after that meeting with the governor.

By 1967, 17 JVS districts had been created or were in the process of being formed. Then in 1968, according to Shoemaker, State Finance Director Howard Collier said, *Byrl, you're not doing this right. There is no plan for the state as a whole. Some districts are going to be left out.*

Shoemaker readily agreed, but had no authority to force any pattern of school district organization. Collier directed him to return within a week with a plan for the ideal plan for vocational education statewide; one that would have the minimum number of vocational planning districts. Collier also wanted projected costs in terms of construction, equipment and operations.

C.O. Tower, assistant director for finance and planning in the Division of Vocational and Career Education, was skilled in computer use and innovation. Employing state-of-the-art technology, he and Shoemaker created eight models with different JVS district configurations. Since the eight largest Ohio cities had sufficient numbers of students and tax bases to support their own vocational education programs, Tower and Shoemaker did not include the major cities in the prototype JVS district state models.

Tower and Shoemaker plotted the state to include all districts in each of the eight models. Costs for construction, equipment and operations were projected for each model. The results revealed that it would take a minimum of 48 JVS districts plus the eight major cities to serve all of Ohio. Construction and equipment costs for the 56 districts were calculated at $350 million. Due to inflation and because the subsequent legislation did not limit the number of vocational districts to 56, the final cost escalated to $600 million.

OHIO ASSOCIATION OF JOINT VOCATIONAL SCHOOL SUPERINTENDENTS

In 1967, the Ohio Association of Joint Vocational School Superintendents (OAJVSS) was organized to represent the interests of the programs, teachers, students and public within the school districts served by the jointures. It provided comprehensive vocational education program opportunities. OAJVSS members worked with the state administration of vocational education to promote vocational education legislation at the state and federal levels. OAJVSS members also consulted with state administrators about their needs and concerns. That organization is still active today under the name of the Ohio Association of Joint Vocational Schools.

AMENDING THE 1963 VOCATIONAL EDUCATION ACT

In 1968, the National Advisory Council for Vocational Education, led by then Ohio Superintendent of Public Instruction Martin Essex, recommended amendments to the 1963 federal *Vocational Education Act*. The committee focused on the social responsibilities of vocational education. The resulting *Vocational Education Amendments of 1968* (PL 90-576) reflected Essex's committee and Congress' concern over the social upheavals of the times.

The amendments authorized millions of dollars for vocational education in the hope of solving the country's social and economic problems. The act also:

1. Created a 21-member national advisory council, with members to be appointed by the President. This council was expected to be influential in future legislation.

2. Created state and local advisory councils to be involved in state and local plan development and to guide vocational education at the state and local school levels.

3. Required much more detailed state plans giving more control over local plans.

4. Earmarked funds for exemplary programs and projects aimed at finding new ways to bridge the gap between school and work. (A focus of the *1994 School to Work Opportunities Act*).

5. Provided funds for state research.

6. Provided funds for programs and projects to broaden or improve vocational education curricula.

7. Provided funds for vocational education leadership and professional development for experienced vocational educators who wanted to engage in full-time training for a period not to exceed three years.

8. Provided funds to support a teacher/industry worker exchange program to update the occupational competencies of vocational teachers.

9. Earmarked funds to support cooperative vocational education programs and cover the additional costs of operating such programs. (Cooperative education programs have been a part of the vocational delivery system for many years and were viewed as essential to a diverse labor market.)

10. Provided funds for consumer and homemaking programs.

11. Provided funds to support work-study programs for needy students.

OHIO COUNCIL ON VOCATIONAL EDUCATION

Amendments to the 1963 *Vocational Education Act* required states to organize state advisory councils with a specified pattern of membership. The amendments provided states with funds to organize and operate such councils. This new mandated advisory council superseded a statewide council Shoemaker had established in 1965. The Ohio Council on Vocational Education (OCOVE) was required to meet at least twice a year. The council was comprised of members representing the interests of agriculture, industry, business, organized labor and vocational education.

The OCOVE was appointed by the State Board of Education. It reported to the state superintendent and the state board, and made recommendations to the board regarding vocational programming in Ohio. Meeting monthly, the council sponsored and directed research studies to assist in the growth and improvement of the state's vocational programs.

Each year OCOVE hosted a public meeting to hear from education, industry and business interests as well as the general public on vocational education successes, issues, and concerns. In preparing its annual report to the state board, the council would use the public statements along with research reports, observations from field visits, and reports requested from the Division of Vocational Education. Twenty two of the 27 OCOVE annual reports are available at the division offices in Columbus. Some of the reports highlight the growth of vocational education; others focus on issues or new developments such as *School to Work*.

The first OCOVE Executive Director was Warren Weiler, former assistant director of agricultural education in the Division of Vocational Education. His successors were John Shannon, former Belmont County and JVS superintendent,

Martin Essex, former state superintendent of public instruction, and Dr. Joseph Davis, former Columbus school superintendent.

In 1998, federal vocational education legislation did not reauthorize state councils on vocational education. Davis finished his term as executive director by writing a history of vocational education and presented it to the state director of vocational education.

SPECIAL NEEDS

As previously noted, the *1968 Vocational Education Amendments* challenged the state education department to create more and better services for disadvantaged and handicapped youth. Dr. Herbert Brum, assistant director for vocational education in the Division of Vocational Education, was appointed as the division's first director of the Special Needs Service. The Special Needs Service focused on programs and services aimed at helping youth with special needs to succeed in a vocational or pre-vocational program.

The 1968 vocational education amendments also reflected the economic and social concerns of the day. Vocational education leaders in Ohio were keenly aware of the growing social problems. They had launched several programs to contribute to their solution. In part, the legislation broadened the focus of vocational education from just meeting existing manpower needs to including the preparation of youth and adults for successful entry into the workforce. The state already had two programs related to that goal.

OHIO'S OCCUPATIONAL WORK EXPERIENCE (OWE) PROGRAM

In 1962, William Dunton, supervisor of T&I education in the Warren City Schools, had developed a program for educationally disenfranchised youth who were economically, academically, and/or socially disadvantaged.

The first class was launched at Market Street High School. Mike Zockle and Don Follett were the teachers. Students were placed in a job requiring limited skills and taught how to keep that job. The students worked a half day on the job and spent the other half day in school where they were enrolled in academic classes and studied with a work-experience coordinator for two periods. The work experience coordinator concentrated on the students' reading, writing, and mathematical skills, as well as work experience and employability skills—the students' attitudes and social habits.

That initiative came to be known statewide as the occupational work experience program (OWE). It was a two-year program planned for students who were in danger of dropping out of school. OWE became part of the regular state vocational education program in 1963. At any point in the program, an OWE student could transfer to a skill-training vocational program or return to the regular academic curriculum. The number of programs and youth enrolled grew rapidly. By 1970 there were 315 OWE programs and more than 6,000 students enrolled statewide. In the 1994-1995 school year, enrollment had jumped to 13,537 students.

Ohio's Occupational Work Adjustment (OWA) Program

In the mid-1960s, Governor Rhodes pointed out to Shoemaker that a number of young people were becoming discouraged with school before they reached the age of 16. Rhodes wanted to lower the age and grade level for student eligibility to enroll in vocational programs. For many young people, high school was the last chance for a full-time education. Historically, vocational programs had been designed for young men and women who were 16 years old or who were in the 11th grade. Experience and research showed that occupational choice did not become reasonable until a young person reached that level of maturity (16 years of age and older). A student could change his or her mind after that age, but changes were less notable.

In 1967, a special vocational education pilot program was authorized by the Ohio Department of Education to serve ninth grade potential dropout students. This pilot program became the first Occupational Work Adjustment (OWA) program, under Brum's direction. The pilot program was conducted at Tallmadge City Schools; John Mensch was the first teacher.

While in school, OWA students would be placed with the program coordinator for two periods and in such other academic classes as they could handle. The program coordinator focused instruction on the basic academic and employability skills that every worker needed for job retention and success. The program coordinator also tutored OWA students in the academic classes in which the students were enrolled. OWA students could transfer to a regular school program at any time that they became motivated to do so. The goal of the program was to get the student into a skill-level training program by age 16, or back into the regular academic main stream. By the 1994-1995 school year, OWA programs across the state enrolled 12,173 students.

The success of the program encouraged changes in federal child labor laws. The Work Experience and Career Exploration Program (WECEP) was established by an amendment to the *Fair Labor Standards Act*. This amendment provided the legal basis for 14 and 15-year-old students to work during school hours. The pilot program was a research experiment. It was originally approved for the period of November 5, 1969 to August 31, 1972 (Federal Register 12892, 1969). On September 3, 1975, the Secretary of Labor amended Child Labor Regulation #3 effective September 4, 1975, to *continue indefinitely on a permanent basis the Work Experience and Career Exploration Program.*

Both the OWE and OWA programs served disadvantaged, mentally and physically challenged, and discouraged youths well. Through these work-based programs, thousands of young people were encouraged to remain in school and to graduate from high school. Joint vocational schools and comprehensive high schools provided opportunities for such young people to remain in school.

Vocational education in Ohio benefited from the additional support provided by the *1968 Vocational Education Amendments.* Although programs were already moving in that direction, the legislation expanded and improved services to special populations throughout the state. After the OWA program was operating effectively, the program was transferred to Dr. Bernard Nye and the Distributive Education Service, which had considerable experience with cooperative education programs. Administrative responsibility for the OWE program was placed with the T&I Service under direction of Assistant Director Harry Davis.

VOCATIONAL EDUCATION FOR THE MENTALLY AND PHYSICALLY CHALLENGED

However, the two programs did not go far enough to meet the needs of disabled and disadvantaged young people who needed special support to succeed in vocational education classes. Teachers needed further development of their skills and attitudes in order to assist and relate to special needs youths.

The *1976 Vocational Education Amendments* further emphasized the need for a more comprehensive program of support and educational services for special needs, and physically and mentally challenged populations. In addition, the *Education for All Handicapped Youth Act* (PL 94-142) provided more funding to state departments of education for special education and vocational education divisions to collaborate on education programs and services for these targeted youth.

Dr. Raymond Horn, director of the Division of Special Education in the Ohio Department of Education, and Shoemaker collaborated closely to better serve the educational and employment needs of these special youths. The Special Education Division assigned a person to initiate and coordinate the two divisions' efforts. The strength of the Vocational and Career Education Division was training youth in the skills, knowledge, work habits and attitudes required for employment. The strength of the Special Education Division was in promoting effective ways to assist special education and vocational education teachers and students in the learning process.

This collaborative effort resulted in three types of services. In some vocational centers, the Special Education Division funded vocational-special education (VOSE) coordinators to enhance occupational training opportunities for special education students. These VOSE coordinators assisted vocational teachers in understanding and effectively accommodating the needs of special education students. The coordinators also worked with individual special education students enrolled in vocational education programs who were encountering difficulties. Option IV, a job placement program for special education students was also introduced in the late 1980s. This program provided low-functioning special education students the opportunity to learn both employment and employability skills that would contribute to their economic independence later in life. Additional information regarding VOSE coordinators and the Option IV program can be found in Chapter XI of this publication.

A third initiative was an in-service training program for vocational education teachers that focused on the skills, attitudes and knowledge that occupational teachers needed to better assist special education students. It was funded by the Division of Vocational Education and provided by the Division of Special Education. More than four hundred vocational teachers received this in-service training.

In a report related to that in-service training, Shoemaker wrote:

> Vocational education must play a larger role in incorporating the disenfranchised—handicapped and/or disadvantaged—into the mainstream of our society. Our institutions—corrective, rehabilitative, jail or courts—are full. Some of these processes have illustrated they do not do the task of "turning people about" to more constructive roles in our society. In other cases, the institution perpetuates the custodial condition that relegates people to stagnation and dependency. Those persons confined under institutional care are liabilities, socially and economically, rather

than assets to productivity. Within education, and vocational education in particular, there must be implemented a viable process for social development and remediation.

In another effort, Richard Macer, who replaced Brum as assistant director in charge of the special needs section in the Division of Vocational Education, and Dr. James J. Buffer Jr. from Cleveland State University published a document entitled *Dimensions of Vocational Education to Serve Special Needs Persons*. Vocational special needs instructors used this manual in their teaching.

The Special Needs Service identified educational problems that made it difficult for students to succeed in vocational programs. The major issues were reading and math rather than discipline or behavior. The service then asked vocational centers to propose projects to deal with the identified problems. Research was conducted over several years on methods of improving reading for special needs students. It was determined that students made more progress when all teachers were provided with workshops on how to teach reading and how to incorporate reading skills improvement into their respective program areas than when a trained reading teacher delivered instruction in a separate class.

With support from the state's special needs unit, Penta County JVS obtained funding from the federal Vocational Rehabilitation Office to build and equip a separate training center for its students with the most severe disabilities. The building included facilities for work assessment and evaluation for any student in the five-county district. In some cases the goal was to train the students to transport themselves to a place of employment and teach them to function in jobs requiring only basic skills. Unfortunately, even though the federal Vocational Rehabilitation Office was extremely satisfied with the services provided by the Penta JVS, it chose not to fund similar training centers in Ohio or throughout the nation.

1967 EDUCATION PROFESSIONS DEVELOPMENT ACT (PL 90-35)

The *Education Professions Development Act (EPDA) of 1967* sought to combine all elements of previous legislation on teacher education into one law. Title V included five personnel preparation programs:

1. National Teacher Corps.

2. Teachers in areas of critical shortage.

3. Fellowships for teachers and other educational professionals.

4. Improved opportunities for training personnel serving in areas other than higher education.

5. Training programs for higher education personnel (and after the passage of 1968 Vocational Education Act Amendments) training for vocational education personnel.

Shoemaker and other vocational education leaders in Ohio recognized that expanding vocational education programs, in both the new JVS districts and major cities, required more leadership personnel, particularly at the local level. In 1966, the Division of Vocational Education created a statewide Leadership Development Program based at Kent State University under the leadership of Dr. Charles Nichols, Kent State's director of the vocational teacher education program. EPDA funds were used to support the leadership development initiative. The program provided participants with knowledge and skills for leadership roles in vocational education. The curriculum and an internship concentrated on leadership rather than administration, and promoted a philosophy of vocational education so that state and local leaders were all moving in the similar directions.

Urban and JVS vocational education planning districts recommended vocational education personnel for the program. The university and the state vocational leadership screened applicants and admitted candidates based upon interests, goals, and admission criteria. The vocational education district that sponsored the prospective candidate agreed to provide the candidate employment for the entire school year so that the candidate would gain experience in a leadership position.

During the summer participants spent full time on the university campus. They participated in classroom discussions and other experiences five days a week for six weeks. After the six-week workshop, participants began their field experiences in their respective school districts. During the school year, there were also regular seminars and the leadership program director made site visits to the interns. The director observed their work, consulted with their supervisors, and counseled each intern.

Program participants received 15 quarter hours of college credit for successfully completing the leadership program. The Division of Vocational Education also partially reimbursed sponsoring districts for the salaries of participants.

Initially, the program, which continued until 1982, was limited to personnel preparing to serve as directors of city or area vocational schools. Later the program was expanded to include candidates preparing to be supervisors for agriculture, business, distributive education, home economics, and T&I education programs. Over time, numerous completers of the Leadership Development Program were appointed to a position of JVS superintendent or other leadership positions in vocational education. During its 17-year history, the program had three directors: Dr. Charles Nichols, Russell Gardner, and Dr. Carl Gorham. Shoemaker, who was state vocational education director throughout the program's life, commented, *Leadership training was the best investment we ever made in vocational education in Ohio.*

EPDA funds were also used to design and implement a plan to evaluate local vocational education programs—*Program Review for Improvement, Development and Expansion* (PRIDE). Congress wanted evidence that vocational education programs were meeting federal standards and were succeeding in preparing young people for work.

Dr. Harold Carr, who later became superintendent of the Great Oaks Institute of Technology and Career Development in southwest Ohio, began developing PRIDE at The Ohio State University as his doctoral dissertation. He completed its development when he was employed in ODE's Division of Vocational Education. The Division of Vocational Education adopted PRIDE in 1968 and used it continuously through 1994.

Finally, EPDA funds made possible improvements in the teacher-learning process in other ways. Shoemaker believed the four factors affecting the quality of vocational programs were staff, student ability and attitudes, facilities and equipment, and curriculum. Through a massive, statewide professional development undertaking, each factor became a major focus for a year.

Beginning in 1977, Dr. Darrell Parks, assistant director for professional development, administered this project. Dr. Lloyd Dull, who had just recently retired as curriculum director for the Akron Public Schools, was employed by the division to assist with this staff development effort. Content experts from around the country were contracted to prepare and present papers on their assigned topics at statewide professional improvement conferences for vocational education teachers and administrators.

Once the papers were written, but before they were presented, Dull prepared analyses and examples of applications of the content in vocational education classrooms and/or laboratories. Also, included with each application were specially designed assessment instruments that teachers could use to measure the respective activities' effectiveness on student learning and performance. These applications also became a part of a series of statewide professional improvement conferences and provided a foundation for rich dialogue among conference participants.

The product of this extensive professional improvement undertaking was the publishing and dissemination of a series of publications entitled *The Heart of Instruction.*

Thirteen separate booklets were published, including:

1. *It Starts with the Teacher*

2. *Psychology of Learning*

3. *Understanding the Adolescent Learner*

4. *Selection and Use of Instructional Resources*

5. *Selection and Use of Teaching Strategies*

6. *Effective Lesson Plans and Assignments*

7. *Teaching Communications Skills*

8. *Relationship of Math and Science Principles to Vocational Curricula*

9. *Classroom Climate for Effective Learning*

10. *Classroom and Laboratory Management*

11. *Techniques of School and Classroom Discipline*

12. *Evaluation of Learning,* and

13. *Leadership for Improved Learning*

Most instructors in T&I education programs entered teaching directly from employment in their skilled occupation. Some of those in agriculture, distributive education, business, and home economics also came from their respective occupations. The monographs provided clear and concise teaching fundamentals for these audiences.

RESEARCH ON STUDENTS' SELF-IMAGE

As the area school concept was initiated in Ohio, a question arose about the effect, positive or negative, of moving students from their home school to a joint vocational school. Some thought separating students from their home school would have a negative effect on those students' self-image.

Dwight A. Pugh, an Ohio University doctoral student, researched the self-image of students at area vocational centers and students at the corresponding home high school. Pugh surveyed students who had just started attending an area vocational school and peer students at the corresponding home schools. Measurements were taken at the beginning of the school year and again four months later.

The study, *A Comparison of Changes over a Period of Time in the Self-Concepts of Students Enrolled in Vocational and Non-Vocational Curricula,* concluded that, in general, vocational students were more open and had a greater capacity for constructive criticism, possessed a higher degree of self-confidence, saw themselves as good, had a higher sense of personal worth, enjoyed a higher feeling of adequacy as a person, and expressed more self-acceptance (self-satisfaction) than non-vocational students.

Vocational education students were also more optimistic, showed less confusion, conflict and contradiction of self-concepts, perceived themselves as more adequate in social interaction, showed fewer signs of maladjustment, and demonstrated less deviance in pre-test, post-test scores than did non-vocational students.

On the other hand, non-vocational students held a lower opinion of themselves, and more often perceived themselves as being outside their own family structure than did vocational students.

GROWTH IN ENROLLMENTS BY 1969

Enrollments in vocational education programs in 1963 were the highest they had ever been, but the numbers still fell far short of meeting the needs of Ohio's growing economy. There were 47,542 students in secondary education programs, 2,122 in post-secondary programs, and 88,589 in adult programs.

The formation of joint vocational school districts and the expansion of vocational education in the major cities resulted in significant increases in enrollments in vocational programs for both youth and adults. Enrollments in 1969 were as follows:

Program Area	High School	Post-Secondary	MDTA*	Extension	Apprentice	Other	Total
Agriculture	15,134	248	76	11,697		25	27,180
Business & Office	17,721	992	1,157	8,446		3,330	31,646
Distributive	8,381	526	61	10,003		487	19,458
Home Economics	54,761	184	20	66,317		442	121,724
Health	1,044	461	49	3,467		3,792	8,813
Trade & Industrial	21,484	2,092	2,552	47,050	10,585	390	84,153
Total	118,525	4,603	3,915	146,980	10,585	8,466	293,974

6

Statewide Planning and Standards for Vocational Education

◆

1969-1983

1969 was a very good year for vocational education in Ohio. Governor James A. Rhodes published a book, *Alternative to a Decadent Society,* setting forth his ideas on the problems in society and the U.S economy. He argued that vocational education should be an integral part of the solution.

Rhodes wrote:

> *Many of today's social and economic ills result from a lack of employment among the able-bodied. This lack of employment stems directly from inadequate education and training. Certain segments of our education are antiquated and obsolete and must be updated if we are to successfully overcome our growing domestic crisis.*

The governor proposed to solve Ohio's social and economic problems with economic development and the jobs that came with growing Ohio's economy. Vocational and technical education would train Ohioans for those jobs.

In 1968, Rhodes appointed a Governor's Task Force on Vocational and Technical Education. The task force was primarily composed of people outside education. Dr. John Ullery of The Ohio State University Hospital in Columbus chaired the task force. When it presented its report in 1969, it strongly supported the expansion and strengthening of vocational and technical education. Since the task force was comprised of non-vocational educators, its recommendations were of even greater significance. In late 1968, Shoemaker told the Ohio Vocational Association Legislative Committee:

> *With the passage of the 1968 Amendments, vocational education will no longer be plagued with initiating 'stop-gap' or band-aid programs on a crisis basis.*
>
> *In Ohio we must strive for three basic goals or concepts which must be realized in the very near future in order to stem the tide of the unemployed and the vocationally unprepared ... The three goals include:*
>
> 1. *A zero dropout rate in vocational education. It is not enough that we educate only those who stay in school. We must make every effort to get the dropout back in school and into some type of education in which he or she can succeed.*
>
> 2. *100% placement of vocational students. Vocational training must be of such a nature as to make its participants readily employable now and in the future.*
>
> 3. *An adequate program of vocational education for all youth in the state of Ohio.*

The goal of providing an adequate program of vocational education for all youth in Ohio seemed unattainable. The development of joint vocational school districts lacked a comprehensive focus. Federal allocations of education funds to the state offered only limited monies to the Division of Vocational Education.

But with the passage of the *1968 Vocational Education Amendments*, a firm foundation was laid for the improvement and expansion of vocational education in Ohio. The 1968 amendments called for business, industry, education, and the general public to evaluate and recommend improvements to the state's vocational programs. In 1969, the State Board of Education appointed the advisory committee for vocational education that had been mandated and funded by the 1968 act. Max Lerner, Lorain Community College president, chaired the initial 22-member committee (Appendix B).

As previously noted, State Finance Director Collier was concerned about the haphazard growth of joint vocational school districts. He once again directed Shoemaker to develop a statewide master plan. The plan proposed a minimum of 48 joint vocational school districts as well as vocational education centers in each of the eight major cities. The cost for implementing the plan was estimated at $350 million for buildings and equipment.

Collier developed the plan details. With the support of Governor Rhodes, the plan received the approval of the General Assembly. It enacted legislation requiring all public school districts to be organized into vocational education planning districts (VEPDs). These VEPDs were to be of sufficient size to provide access to an adequate program of vocational education for all 11th and 12th grade students enrolled in public education.

> *This was landmark legislation,* recalled Shoemaker. *No state in the nation had ever attempted to require that vocational education be made available to all students, including a specified number of program offerings to meet state standards.*

Shoemaker worked with the governor's office and the legislature in the development and passage of the legislation, but it was the work of Governor Rhodes and Collier that were the determining forces.

One significant provision in the legislation stipulated the minimum number of students required in the upper four grades for a school district to qualify as a stand-alone vocational education planning district. Shoemaker recommended that no district should plan alone unless it enrolled a minimum of 2,500 students in grades 9-12. The bill passed the House and Senate with that provision, but in conference committee a local school superintendent from a small city that had only 1,500 students in the upper four grades persuaded a prominent legislator to lower the figure to 1,500. *We will never know what would have happened if the number had stayed at 2,500,* Shoemaker ruefully noted.

By April 1, 1970, all city, exempted, and local school districts were required to develop and submit plans to the State Board of Education that met both the provisions of the law and the standards established by the board.

At the same time, Governor Rhodes proposed, and Ohio voters approved, a major bond issue. It included $75 million for vocational education. Initially $25 million had been planned, but a second provision enabled the legislature to provide construction funds to higher education during each biennium. At the request of the governor, the chancellor for higher education released some funds initially proposed for higher education for use in vocational education.

Shoemaker noted, however, that $75 million would not provide the funds required for the construction and equipment needs for all the planned vocational facilities. Also, there was a major step between the requirement of a plan and the implementation of a plan. The law called for state standards for vocational education, and assigned the responsibility for setting those standards to the State Board of Education.

With the added responsibilities assigned to the Division of Vocational Education, Shoemaker charged D.R. Purkey, an assistant supervisor in the Agricultural Education Service, to lead the implementation of the statewide plan.

One of Purkey's first assignments was to draft vocational education standards for consideration by the state superintendent and the State Board of Education. Once the standards were drafted, State Superintendent Martin Essex requested the Division of Vocational Education to hold public hearings on the draft in four sections of the state. Dr. Franklin Walter, deputy superintendent of public instruction, accompanied division staff to give advice and counsel at the hearings. As a result of the public hearings, minor revisions were made in the standards. They were then presented to the state superintendent for adoption by the State Board of Education.

Although the general public seemed to be receptive, Shoemaker recalled that there was massive resistance from superintendents across the state. They felt threatened by the loss of authority and the State Board's intent to make major changes affecting the autonomy of their school districts. Pressure was exerted on the state superintendent to reduce the standards, but Essex never requested the Division of Vocational Education to change them.

The standards were presented to the State Board at its January 1970 meeting. The board held the meeting in the largest hearing room in the department building. About 500 superintendents attended the hearing, the majority of whom opposed the standards. The hearing lasted from 1 p.m. until 11 p.m.

At one point a superintendent who opposed the standards was going up and down the aisle encouraging the opposition, said Shoemaker.

At the hearing's conclusion, the board reconvened in its regular meeting room and proceeded to vote. Neither the superintendent, nor any member of the state staff was asked to make a statement. Shoemaker recalled that the board members were allowed to vote their beliefs.

Each of the standards was voted on separately; each passed, 11 to 9. Although the vote was close, the standards were adopted. Shoemaker noted:

> *It was to the credit of the state board that once the standards were passed, state board members never referred to the vote. Every member supported the board's decision. The decision may have been unpopular among many of the superintendents, but it proved quite acceptable to the voters over the state.*

Major provisions in the standards included:

1. Districts were required to provide vocational education to meet the vocational education standards by 1974.

2. Plans were required to provide no less than 12 different offerings and 20 classes under the school foundation program.

3. Vocational Education Planning Districts (VEPDs) had to have a minimum of 1,500 students in the upper four grades.

4. Districts could meet the requirements by:

    a. forming a joint vocational school district;

    b. contracting between districts with one district providing not less than 10 programs and 16 classes, with participating districts required to enroll or pay for a minimum number of students;

    c. enrolling 1,500 or more students in the upper four grades, and offering at least 12 vocational education programs and 20 vocational classes.

As required by law, local plans were submitted by April 1, 1970. At that time there were 638 school districts in the state. Plans called for the formation of 126 VEPDs. Purkey and Dr. Darrell Parks, the assistant supervisor for agriculture, reviewed each plan for compliance with the standards. A list of all approved VEPD plans was reported in the Ohio Department of Education newsletter in June 1970. (The VEPD plans, in many cases, were tentative at best. The goal of an adequate program for all youth in the state was not achieved until 1983.)

In 1968, there were 10 JVS districts in operation, Springfield-Clark County, Eastland at Groveport, EHOVE (for Erie, Huron and Ottawa Counties), Four County (Defiance, Fulton, Henry, and Williams Counties), Greene County, Lake County, Penta County (Lucas, Wood, Sandusky, Erie, and Ottawa Counties), Pike County, Sandusky County (which later changed its name to Vanguard JVS district), and Tri-County in Nelsonville (Athens, Hocking, Perry Counties).

By the early 1970s, the number of joint vocational school districts had doubled. The new JVS districts included Ashtabula, Belmont, Hamilton, Knox, Lorain, Mahoning, Montgomery, South Central Cuyahoga, Washington, and Wayne counties.

In 1973, the General Assembly gave the State Board authority to assign school districts to JVS districts or to contractual arrangements. That legislation stimulated the growth of vocational education. The number of JVS districts increased, as did the number of youth and adults served.

IMPLEMENTING THE PLANS

There was a massive amount of work to be accomplished in moving the plans from the paper on the table to active and effective programs serving the youth and adults, recalled Shoemaker.

Shoemaker had promised Governor Rhodes and the members of the General Assembly the vocational centers would serve more adults in retraining and upgrading programs than were served at the high school level. It was understood that classes for adults would not be of the length of those provided for the youth. When funds were awarded to planning districts for construction and equipment costs, the districts agreed to provide programs for adults as well as high school youth.

But funds from the Rhodes administration bond issue were depleted by the early 1970s. There was not enough available money in federal funds to cover all the requests. In the meantime, control of the state legislature and the governor's office changed from the Republican Party to the Democratic Party in 1970. John Gilligan became governor, but the change in leadership did not affect bi-partisan legislative support for vocational education. As the statewide plan for vocational education evolved, the legislature continued to vote the necessary funds. *It was awkward for members of the legislature to refuse to provide the funds for another district,* noted Shoemaker, *when the district they represented had already received funds.*

The majority of local school districts across the state organized into JVS districts. A few organized as contract districts. There were also a number of city districts. Winning voter approval for the required local funding was easy in some districts, and difficult in others. One county superintendent, who had taken the lead in forming a JVS district, went to the voters seven times before they finally passed the property tax levy. In two regions of northwest Ohio there was organized resistance. One of those regions challenged the "JVS Law" in the courts but the challenge was denied.

From 1963 to 1983 approximately $550 million were spent by VEPDs on facilities and equipment. Approximately half the funds came from the state, or were federal funds allocated by the state. Purkey managed the allocation of federal funds. After Purkey retired in 1971, Frank Oliverio managed fund allocation and reviewed construction plans.

From the outset, the Division of Vocational Education sought to get the most construction for the money. The division decided not to develop a design pattern for the construction of facilities. Instead, the division required only that there be a minimum number of square feet of usable floor space in relationship to the amount of money allocated. This forced architects to consider the most efficient designs in the construction of vocational facilities. Shoemaker said:

> *They screamed about the floor space required in relation to the money allotted, but we held firm. No person in the division ever drew a line on a plan, but every architectural plan was reviewed in accordance with pre-determined design concepts and cost-saving ideas. Architects finally understood the process, and Ohio vocational buildings were built at significantly less cost than other school buildings.*

VOCATIONAL EDUCATION IN THE MAJOR CITIES

According to the state standards, Ohio's eight major cities had more than enough students to establish more than adequate programs of vocational education. As the effort to provide an adequate program for all youth in the state was developed, each of the major cities planned for the building of vocational high schools or addition of vocational facilities to existing high schools.

Even though some individual city high schools had 1,500 or more students in grades 9-12, the districts determined that they could provide a broader vocational education program by bringing students together at a vocational center. In addition to business education, distributive education, health occupations, and the skilled trades, the major cities' participation in the growth of vocational education included programs in agriculture and home economics. The following summarizes the growth of vocational education in Ohio's eight major cities.

Akron

Hower Vocational High School was the center for vocational education in Akron. No new buildings were added for vocational education, but some facilities were remodeled and expanded. No agriculture programs were added, but significant programs in vocational home economics were added to the curriculum in a number of high schools.

One experimental home economics program in Akron was a pre-school program for children from homes where both parents were deaf or could not speak. The children did not talk when they first came to the classes, but rather quickly learned to act as normal children when given a socially stimulating environment.

Another innovative program provided educational services to youths who were in serious problems in their home schools. The program was offered in a camp setting in a wooded area of the city. The contact with nature seemed to have a therapeutic affect on the students. One instructor explained, *When we first looked over the grounds around the classrooms, if the students saw something move they would kill it and then ask what it was. After a while they stopped the killing, and asked what it was.*

Canton

In 1939, the Timken Foundation built an outstanding vocational education high school—Timken Vocational High School—for the Canton City School District. The elderly H.H. Timken, chairman of The Timken Company, was taken on a tour through the new building. In the early 1960s, the Timken Foundation completely updated the equipment in the building. Canton did not need new or additional facilities, but some new programs were added at Canton McKinley High School.

Timken Vocational High School long served as a drawing card for some of the best students in the city. The Timken Company and other industries in the area, such as the Hoover Company, provided good jobs for the graduates. Often notices of promotions in the Timken Company would note the person graduated from the Timken Vocational High School.

Cincinnati

Herman Schneider, a University of Cincinnati professor, had a marked effect on the vocational programs in the Cincinnati public schools. Initially most vocational education programs in the city were cooperative in design. Students went to school for a part of the school day, then worked in business or industry for an equal period of time.

In 1955, using local tax revenues, Superintendent Claude Courter built a large vocational center, Central Vocational High School. As a result, Cincinnati did not need to add facilities when the state began expanding vocational education. C.O. Tower, who had been in the Cincinnati Public Schools central office, and Ruth Lape, who had headed the girls vocational school, were the first administrators of Central Vocational High School.

The facility was, however, not located in the center of the city and transportation was not provided for the students. The transportation problem had a negative effect on the enrollment at Central Vocational. The school was sold in the 1970s for use as a technical institute. The administration used funds from the sale of Central Vocational High School to add vocational facilities to various city high schools and to transport students between schools. The vocational programs and the Vocational Industrial Clubs of America youth organization became popular in Cincinnati. Enrollments grew in the early 1970s; however, racial desegregation issues led to a decline in enrollments in the late 1970s.

Cleveland

In the 1950s, Cleveland had, on its own, built two new vocational high schools—Max S Hayes for boys and Jane Addams for girls. (The names were the same names as the old Cleveland vocational schools.) Labor unions and the business community supported new construction to provide training for apprentices. Apprentices were required to receive classroom instruction of no less than four hours per week, including mathematics, science, and technology related to their respective craft areas.

When Paul Briggs became superintendent in Cleveland, he complained that Cleveland was not getting its fair share of funds from the vocational education division in Columbus. Briggs, who had been superintendent for five years in Parma, as well as in Michigan, arrived in Cleveland with the full support of the city power structure, including the news media.

The Cleveland news media publicized his complaints. In an editorial one newspaper referred to "that little tin God in Columbus"—a reference to Vocational Education Division Director Shoemaker. In 1963, over a period of six Saturdays citizens from Cleveland met with Governor Rhodes and Shoemaker to underscore Briggs' concerns. Shoemaker responded that Cleveland was getting its fair share.

According to Shoemaker, Briggs stated he would never build another vocational high school in Cleveland. Eventually, Briggs' complaints about funding were investigated by the federal government. The investigators concluded that Cleveland was getting its fair share. That ended the complaints and also launched what Shoemaker called a relationship of excellent cooperation between Briggs and the Division of Vocational Education. *Dr. Briggs and I became the best of friends*, said Shoemaker. *He was an outstanding superintendent.*

Briggs embarked on a massive building campaign. He established vocational programs in each new high school. Briggs also focused on the two vocational high schools, making them the elite vocational programs in the city. Later, however, he found that some areas of vocational education could not be justified in each high school. Cleveland then built an aviation vocational high school and a health occupations high school. *Briggs probably built the finest major city vocational program in the nation,* Shoemaker stated.

In 1982, 65% of all juniors and seniors enrolled in the Cleveland high schools were in job-training vocational programs. Another 10% were in vocational home economics. Cleveland also had the largest agricultural education program in Ohio. It included off-farm agriculture programs, such as greenhouse production, landscape design, installation and maintenance, and floriculture.

Realizing that city youth needed instruction related to home life in the areas of child care, money management, and home management, Cleveland undertook such programs. One experimental program in the inner-city poverty areas provided home instruction to mothers of children from birth to three years. This program was based on research that indicated that the period of birth through two years of age was the most important learning period of a child's life.

The racial desegregation movement of the 1980s had the unintended result of undermining the vocational programs in most of Ohio's major cities, but Cleveland was probably affected the most. Briggs argued for maintaining the program offerings and locations that he had instituted, but the federal courts disagreed. Subsequently, Briggs retired.

Columbus

Until 1970, the Columbus City Schools system did not have any programs at the high school level that met state standards for vocational education. There was a building on Spring Street identified as a trade school, but it was a less than adequate facility. Central High School had a large number of industrial arts facilities and business programs, but the short time allotted to the curriculum and the limited equipment in some programs prevented them from qualifying for vocational education funding.

When Harold Eibling became Columbus superintendent, he invited Shoemaker to visit Central High School to determine whether it could be made into a vocational center. Shoemaker said the industrial arts teachers appeared to be certifiable to teach vocational programs and were very interested in having their programs meet vocational standards. The industrial arts director made it very clear, however, that he did not want to have the programs meet vocational standards, recalled Shoemaker.

Later Eibling met with Shoemaker to request a survey of business and industry to determine interest in establishing vocational programs. The school district's central staff, however, did not support the idea; the survey was never completed.

In the early 1970s, a new superintendent, John Ellis, discussed with Shoemaker the possibility of building vocational facilities at four sites. Three would be new facilities. They would be located in different geographic areas of the city, and each would provide somewhat different curricula. The fourth would be a combination of remodeled buildings and a new facility on the site of the Fort Hayes Army Reserve Center. Depending on their occupational goals, students would be permitted to attend any one of the career centers.

Shoemaker suggested that the centers be career academies. They would include both vocational programs and redesigned pre-professional programs built around the broad goals of engineering and science, business, health, and social sciences. Ellis was interested, but indicated he could not get the support to implement such a concept.

Still, Ellis overcame years of lethargy in the system. Winning public support, he built the four vocational centers—the Northeast Career Center, the Northwest Career Center, the Southeast Career Center, and the Fort Hayes Career Center.

One of the curricular offerings at Fort Hayes was an exemplary program in the performing arts. Program areas included music, dance and drama. Leslie Susi, a band teacher in the Columbus school system and a member of the local musicians' union, organized the program. Students were enrolled on the basis of auditions. Many of the program graduates were employed in the performing arts profession.

Jack Gibbs, an exemplary administrator at the Fort Hayes Career Center, was planning to work with Shoemaker to make Fort Hayes a Career Academy, but Gibbs met an untimely death before the plan could be fulfilled.

Dayton

Dayton Public Schools had a long history of vocational education at both the high school and adult levels. Over the years, Dayton probably had the largest adult program of any of the major cities, as well as the closest relationship with industry. The high schools' vocational facilities were used for adults, but the public schools' vocational programs were mostly offered on site at the many industries. Paul Snyder, the Dayton City Schools vocational director, proved to be a capable leader and was very instrumental in the success of the Dayton City Schools vocational education program.

Dayton had built a new facility, Patterson Cooperative High School, before state and federal funds became available for construction and equipment. The vocational programs at Dayton Patterson were unique. Students attended the vocational school for two weeks; then they worked in business or industry full time for two weeks. The program ran through the summer to assure enough time for related technical and academic classes. The cooperative plan of training at Patterson Cooperative High School maintained a close relationship with the local business and industrial community.

The city also built a high school facility for a career academy; offering a re-designed, pre-professional program built around the areas of engineering sciences, business, health, and the social sciences. However, the school never became operational in accordance with the purpose for which it was originally designed.

Vocational education opportunities grew rapidly. A 1970-71 issue of the school system's weekly publication *School-day* reported that *for the first time in the history of Dayton schools, teachers and students return this week to classrooms that offer job preparation in every high school.* There were 127 job-preparation classes, nearly double the 72 classes that were offered the previous year. More than a fourth of the city's high school students were enrolled in vocational education classes.

Toledo

Toledo had a long and rich history of maintaining excellent vocational programs for both youth and adults at Macomber Vocational High School for boys and Whitney Vocational High School for girls. These two schools stood next to each other near the center of the city. Both schools had excellent reputations with young people as well as with business and industry. Frederick M. Dannenfelser at Macomber and Ethel Wooden at Whitney ran the schools with very strict hands; Dannenfelser was often at odds with the central administration, according to Shoemaker.

When Frank Dick became Toledo superintendent the early 1960s, he began a program to racially integrate the schools. He built vocational facilities and added programs, including agriculture and home economics, in several of the high schools. The additions included in-school home economics programs and the adult and child-care programs like those offered in Cleveland. Toledo also began busing students from one high school to vocational programs in another. At its peak, job-training vocational education in Toledo enrolled 60% or more of the juniors and seniors. Additional students were enrolled in vocational home economics. Spreading vocational programs across the city did not, however, end the desegregation issues. Emphasis on vocational programs was seriously eroded over time. Macomber and Whitney eventually closed.

Youngstown

As funds became available for new facilities, the Youngstown Board of Education decided to build a new vocational high school, Choffin Career Center. The new center was well-accepted by the community and provided improved opportunities for job training to both youth and adults. A horticulture program was added at the career center. Vocational home economics classes were added to the curriculum in the high schools throughout the city.

Youngstown's programs were not as affected by the desegregation movement of the late 1970s as some of the larger school systems. In the early 1980s, nearly 60% of the 11th and 12th grade students in the city were enrolled in job-training programs.

GROWTH AND STATE BOARD SUPPORT

In 1982, 42% of all public school high school juniors and seniors in Ohio were enrolled in job-training programs. Another 13% were enrolled in vocational home economics (work and family-life programs). Enrollments in job-training programs in the major cities approached or exceeded 60%. The 1981 State Board's Report, which listed goals for educational programs, stated:

> *Enrollment and sex equity in job training vocational programs will increase by 2% per year through 1984-85 without undue pressure to meet quotas.*

Other goals for vocational education stated in the report included the following:

1. *The average scores of senior students in vocational education, except those enrolled in Occupational Work Experience (OWA), on standardized achievement tests in reading and math will equal or exceed the state or national norms by June 1984.*

2.   *At least 12,000 eligible students will be enrolled in OWA programs by September 1985, and such students will be motivated to remain in school.*

3.   *At least 96% of the graduates from vocational education job-training programs available for placement will be employed, with at least 60% placement in a field related to training, by July 1985.*

Ohio's vocational education program met or exceeded the state board goals.

COMPLETING THE JOB OF PROVIDING AN ADEQUATE PROGRAM FOR ALL YOUTH

By 1982 all the state, except for two areas in northwestern Ohio, had funded joint vocational school districts, completed their buildings, and were in operation. The 49 districts in operation were:

Apollo (Lima), Ashland County-West Holmes (Ashland), Ashtabula County (Jefferson), Auburn (Concord Township), Belmont-Harrison (St. Clairesville), Buckeye (New Philadelphia), Butler County (Hamilton), Central Ohio (Plain City), Columbiana County (Lisbon), Coshocton County (Coshocton), Cuyahoga Valley (Brecksville),

Delaware (Delaware), Eastland (Groveport), EHOVE (Milan), Four County (Archbold), Gallia-Jackson-Vinton (Rio Grand), Great Oaks Institute of Technology and Career Development (Cincinnati), Greene County (Xenia), Jefferson County (Bloomingdale), Knox County (Mt Vernon), Lawrence County (Chesapeake), Licking County (Newark),

Lorain County (Oberlin), Mahoning County (Canfield), Maplewood Area (Ravenna), Medina County (Medina), Miami Valley Career Tech (Clayton), Mid-East Ohio (Zanesville), Ohio Hi-Point (Bellefontaine), Penta County (Perrysburg), Pickaway-Ross County (Chillicothe), Pike County Area (Piketon), Pioneer Career & Technology (Shelby), Polaris (Middleburg Heights), Portage Lakes (Green), Scioto County (Lucasville),

Southern Hills (Georgetown), Springfield-Clark (Springfield), Stark County Area (Massillon), Tri-County (Nelsonville), Tri-Rivers (Marion), Trumbull County (Warren), U.S. Grant (Bethel), Upper Valley (Piqua), Vanguard-Sentinel (Fremont), Vantage (Van Wert), Warren County (Lebanon), Washington County (Marietta), and Wayne County (Smithville).

CHANGE IN LEADERSHIP

Shoemaker retired June 30, 1982, having served as director for 20 years. The goal of an adequate vocational program for all youth was more than 95% complete. What had been only a dream in 1957—when an experimental area school started in Pike County—was in sight. Dr. Darrell Parks was appointed to the position of state director of vocational education and took over on July 1, 1982.

State Superintendent Frank Walter directed Parks to make it his number one priority to complete the statewide plan for vocational education by bringing into compliance the remaining local districts that were not a part of an official VEPD. Included in this group were local schools in Auglaize, Darke, Fairfield, Hancock, Paulding, and Mercer counties.

Hancock and Paulding local schools formalized a contractual agreement with the Findlay City Schools and formed the Millstream Vocational Education Compact. The local boards of education in Darke County petitioned the Montgomery County Joint Vocational School (now the Miami Valley Career Technology Center) Board of Education for membership in that JVS district and were accepted. Auglaize and Mercer County schools formed the Tri-Star Compact with the central vocational education facility being located in the Celina City Schools. The local schools in Fairfield petitioned for membership into the Eastland Joint Vocational School District. It is now called the Eastland-Fairfield Joint Vocational School District.

With one exception, the voters in each planning district where vocational facility construction was required, approved local tax issues to support the vocational programs. One planning district was able to get state funding without local matching funds. The goal of providing an adequate program of vocational education for all youth in the state had been achieved.

7

Vocational Education Program Areas

This chapter addresses the five traditional program areas of vocational education. Other important and significant program initiatives that were integral to Ohio's vocational education history are addressed in other chapters. For example, Veteran's Training programs and services are discussed in Chapter II, and the Special Needs programs are a part of Chapter V.

Chapter IX is dedicated to Vocational Education for Adults. Chapter X discusses career choice and Ohio's Career Education program. JTPA/Jobs for Ohio Graduates, Sex Equity/ONOW, Applied Academics, and Tech Prep comprise a major portion of Chapter XI.

AGRICULTURAL EDUCATION
Contributed by Darrell Parks

The vocational agriculture movement officially began in the early 1920s, but Elyria High School introduced the first secondary agricultural program in 1902. That same year A.B. Graham initiated a program of instruction in agriculture in Clark County's Springfield Township School, where he was superintendent.

In 1911, the General Assembly passed an act making the teaching of agriculture mandatory in both elementary and high schools in rural and village districts. Although the instruction was general rather than vocational in nature, this was the beginning of an agricultural education program in Ohio, a program that thrived and established itself throughout the state.

The Vocational Agriculture Program

On February 23, 1917, Congress approved the *Smith-Hughes Act*, which provided for vocational agriculture training in grades below college level. The *Smith-Hughes Act* was instrumental in the evolution of a new educational concept: The school, the vocation, and the home farm were integrated. Students learned technical knowledge in agriculture and applied it on home farm enterprises in which they had financial and management interests. In vocational agriculture vernacular it was known as "learning by doing." Although some questioned the validity of the concept in the beginning, it created an effective learning environment. Today that same concept is referred to as applied or contextual learning. It is recognized as an effective teaching and learning process in various educational settings.

Throughout its early years, vocational agriculture focused upon preparing high school-aged students and adults to become better farmers. The formative years of vocational agriculture coincided with World War I when food production was of major importance.

After World War II, however, a rapidly changing economy and employment pattern called for a change in vocational agriculture. The program became more than just about farming. As off-farm business interests took over operations once performed on the farm, it was recognized that workers in these enterprises needed and could benefit from skills in agriculture.

In 1956, P. D. Wickline launched a pilot program in landscape design at Xenia High School. In 1957, Dr. Herbert Brum completed a major study that identified a need for specialized instruction in off-farm agricultural occupations. Concurrently, similar discussions about expanding vocational agriculture beyond the scope of farming were taking place nationally. As a strong agribusiness industry emerged, it required trained agriculturalists.

With the passage of the *1963 Vocational Education Act*, a new era began for agricultural education. The program expanded from rural and exempted village school districts to suburban and urban districts. Agricultural education became an integral part of the joint vocational school movement in Ohio. For the first time, female high school students were admitted to the program.

There was a great expansion in the late 1960s and 1970s. Under the direction of James E. Dougan, state agricultural education director from 1969 to 1979, eight program areas were developed. These programs included production agriculture, forestry, ornamental horticulture, agricultural and industrial equipment and service, resource conservation, environmental management, agricultural products processing, and agricultural business and service.

In 1962, the Cleveland school system established the first city vocational agriculture department, marking the advent of major city vocational agriculture and the Future Farmers of America (FFA). The Cleveland program grew steadily to become the largest urban-center agricultural education program in the nation. Today there are more than 350 agricultural education programs throughout the state, serving approximately 23,000 secondary education students.

FFA (Future Farmers of America)

By 1922, most vocational agriculture students belonged to local agriculture clubs led by their vocational instructors. These clubs offered rural students the opportunity to develop their organizational and leadership abilities, as well as additional personal, social, and civic skills. Many of these clubs had well-planned programs. Activities included parent-son banquets, pest hunts, and school fairs. Community service and fund-raising projects such as seed corn testing, custom spraying, and cooperative broiler and orchard projects were popular. Many clubs sponsored trips to the state fair for livestock judging and to the Agricultural Experiment Station in Wooster.

In November 1928, Ray Fife, state vocational agriculture supervisor, asked R. B. Warner, vocational agriculture teacher at Ashley and one of his outstanding students, to represent Ohio at a meeting in Kansas City, Missouri, at which the national Future Farmers of America organization was launched. That meeting combined with the agriculture club movement to give birth to the Ohio FFA Association on February 28, 1929. The first state organizational meeting of the FFA took place February 7-8 in University Hall on The Ohio State University campus. Eighty delegates from 52 chapters took part. Ralph Howard served as temporary chairman. Bylaws were adopted, and Larry Augenstein, Ohio's student representative at the Kansas City meeting, became the first Ohio FFA president.

On May 31, 1929, delegates attending the first Ohio FFA Association State Convention elected a full slate of officers. They included President Ralph Bender from Waldo, Vice President John C. North from Madison, Secretary Raymond Dellinger from Hilliard, Treasurer Robert Lane from Marietta, Reporter Paul Hartsook from Worthington, Advisor Ray Fife from Columbus, and Executive Secretary-Treasurer Ralph Howard from Columbus. The convention voting body approved some changes to the constitution and increased annual state dues from 20 cents to 30 cents. Within three years, state-sponsored activities included a public speaking contest, a newsletter, the sending of delegates to the national convention, the honoring of outstanding Ohio farmers, the nomination of American Farmer candidates, and exhibits at the state fair.

In 1933, Bobby Jones was elected national FFA president, the third Ohio FFA member to hold a national office. (Lawrence Augenstein and Ralph Bender served as national officers in 1929 and 1930 respectively.) As national president, Jones traveled through the western states and to Hawaii, a territory that had a very active FFA Association. The Ohio Association voted to pay "any amount needed" up to $50 toward Jones' expenses for the Hawaiian trip. In all, there have been 29 national FFA officers from Ohio, the largest number of national officers from any state.

In its first 25 years, the Ohio FFA Association had three adult leaders who served as executive secretaries. They included Ralph Howard, Warren G. Weiler, and D. R. Purkey. Since then, Earl F. Kantner, Robin C. Hovis, Jim Scott, and Steve Gratz have served as executive secretaries of the state association.

Another hallmark of Ohio's rich FFA history is the blue and gold FFA jacket. In 1933, the Fredericktown FFA Band, considered by many to be the first "National FFA Band," was preparing for the national FFA convention in Kansas City. Fredericktown agriculture instructor Julius "Gus" Lintner was concerned about the band members' outerwear. He thought winter coats would be too warm; yet the students needed something that would be warm—and would also distinguish them as band members.

Lintner recalled:

> One evening as I passed the local clothing store, I noticed some corduroy jackets displayed with different colors and emblems. I went in and asked where they were made, how much they cost and whether the FFA emblem could be used? The following week Mr. A. Tolan of the Universal Uniform Company, Van Wert, Ohio called on me. I showed him the official emblem. He assured me that the emblem could be a part of the jacket. The total cost would be $5.50 per jacket. I was concerned about the positioning of the emblem, and how the lettering would look on the back of the jacket.
>
> At a meeting with parents, I showed them the jacket and how it could be used for school as well as for the home. The parents accepted my plan. Thirty-five jackets were ordered using the original emblem.

The jacket's blue and gold has become FFA's trademark. FFA members throughout the United States have bought more than four million jackets.

Through the years, the FFA has seen many changes and innovations. During the 1950s and 1960s, Ohio's FFA membership grew at the rate of about 1,000 per year. By the end of the century it stood at 21,868. In 1964, on the advice of legal counsel and with national FFA Association's approval, young women became official Ohio FFA members.

Perhaps one of the most dramatic events occurred when the state FFA advisory committee, at its February 1974 meeting, sought approval from the Ohio Vocational Agriculture Teachers Association (OVATA) to select and recognize FFA state degree recipients by taxonomy. The OVATA executive committee, chaired by President Jack Devitt, approved the request. Forms were developed and distributed in 1975 for the first State FFA Degree candidates by taxonomy.

FFA Camp Muskingum was incorporated December 18, 1941, as the Ohio Future Farmers of America Camps, Inc. Located on 160 acres of rolling land on the eastern shore of the Muskingum Conservancy District's Leesville Lake in Carroll County, the camp promotes conservation education, leadership training, and outdoor recreation. Through the year 2000, 63,357 FFAers had attended Camp Muskingum.

The Ohio FFA Center, located on the grounds of the Ohio Exposition Center in Columbus, was completed in 1986. The first such center in the nation, the 6,000-square-foot structure is the repository for FFA records and memorabilia. It includes a Hall of Achievement, visual displays, and historical documents.

Adult Farmer Education

Vocational agriculture, now known as agricultural education, was not limited to secondary programs in public schools. Recognizing the importance of keeping pace with the latest advances in agricultural science and approved farming practices, local departments offered evening adult classes for those involved with farming.

Class topics ranged from animal husbandry and crop production to the marketing of farm products and the latest farm management practices. The local vocational agriculture teacher coordinated the adult program, often providing the instruction, but frequently calling upon the assistance of county extension agents or agribusiness representatives. The instruction was usually free to the attendees, but dues were sometimes collected to defray mailing costs and refreshments.

Statewide participation in adult classes exceeded 20,000 a year. The weekly classes ranged from 15-20 participants and lasted for one and a half to two hours. Classes were most often offered during the winter months when farmers were not involved with the seasonal activities of planting and harvesting crops.

During World War II, vocational agriculture teachers organized farm labor training and food production classes. The Food for Victory program, also known as Good Production War Training, resulted in 8,000 farm machines being repaired under the supervision of vocational agricultural teachers. Many of these teachers taught in two departments as other teachers joined the Armed Forces.

Following World War II, the veterans training program flourished through efforts of vocational agriculture and veterans training teachers. This institutional, on-farm training program was designed to prepare veterans for farm operation and ownership. It was a strong program in Ohio. More than 500 teachers and 11,000 veterans took part at 400 school sites. The program ended in the early 1950s.

The Young Farmer Association

Young farmers were frequently confronted with problems different from those of older, more established farmers. Besides production and management challenges, younger farmers took on additional burdens of land acquisition, and equipment and livestock purchases. These often created high debt obligations and difficulties in maintaining a cash flow sufficient to provide operating capital.

As early as 1921, State Supervisor Ray Fife submitted a plan to the State Board of Vocational Education. It proposed *Part-time Instruction* for young farmers. As recorded in *Education for Agriculture, A History of the Ohio Vocational Agriculture Teachers Association—1925-1975*(p. 93):

> *The first short course especially for young farmers was offered by W. F. Bruce of Hamilton Township, Franklin County, in 1922. Bruce found that his students wanted to do more than have agriculture meetings. They wanted to visit each other's farms, to take field trips to agricultural cooperatives, to play basketball, and to hold picnics, parties and social affairs. He accordingly developed such a program to supplement his short course and met with much success. Bruce also surveyed the possibilities of similar programs in other vocational agriculture departments and published his results in 1925.*

This study received much attention during the next five years as the young farmer program expanded. By 1928, 55 departments were offering part-time courses for young farmers, and the program continued to grow. In 1941, there were 222 young farmer programs enrolling more than 4,500 members. Unfortunately, World War II greatly curtailed the programs; by 1945 there were only 722 young farmer members in the state.

After the war interest in a young farmer program revived. The program received support from regional vocational agriculture specialists in the U. S. Office of Education. They promoted a *complete program of vocational agriculture* to include three groups—high school students, young farmers and adult farmers. In 1948, Floyd J. Ruble, a member of the state vocational agricultural supervisory staff, launched the Ohio Young Farmer program. It focused on farmers who had just finished high school up to 30 years of age.

The first *Ohio Young Farmer Manual* was prepared by Ralph E. Bender. It included a draft copy of the first constitution and bylaws of the Ohio Association of Young Farmers of America (YFA) that was adopted March 3, 1951. Early state YFA leaders were Floyd J. Ruble and H.D. Brum. They served respectively as association executive secretaries through 1984. Their successors were Richard Hummel and John Miley.

In 1958, acknowledging that farming was mainly a husband/wife partnership, the association began holding an annual two-day state convention with programs for wives. In time the association officially changed its name to the Ohio Young Farmer/Young Farm Wives Association.

Over more than 30 years, the Ohio YFA expanded. Contributions from the agricultural business and industry community made possible an awards program. Other activities included area tours, leadership conferences, an annual state YFA camp program at FFA Camp Muskingum, and a quarterly state newsletter. YFA's statewide membership peaked at 2,600 in the late 1980s.

BUSINESS AND OFFICE EDUCATION (BOE)
Contributed by Robert Balthaser

Since the beginning of recorded history there have been occupations related to business. However, education of office workers began in earnest in the 1800s after E. Remington & Sons introduced the Sholes and Glidden Type Writer. Public educators left their schools to start business colleges to offer instruction in the use of these newfangled machines.

In response to public pressure, schools initiated courses in shorthand and typing, although sometimes only as post high school offerings. Then colleges began training business teachers. Demand for business instruction first brought courses into the high schools and then into the junior high schools. The approach was, however, a cafeteria approach. Students took only what they wanted rather than a comprehensive program based on employment standards. As one employer stated, *They can type OK, but they cannot work at a desk, nor do they have any idea how to.*

With the advent of <u>vocational</u> business programs, full-size office training class-rooms and laboratories equipped like real business offices in the private sector became the standard. Anita Oglesby, a business teacher at Bellefontaine High School, who had received a grant from the Sloan Foundation, consulted with the state Division of Vocational Education on new equipment for her program. The Sloan Foundation had provided her with a grant to supplement school district funds. Thus, Bellefontaine High School acquired Ohio's first modernly equipped BOE classroom and laboratory and set the standard for the state.

Colleges and universities trained teachers in the art of teaching. But the business community provided committees to help business teachers determine course content and procedures. Programs were also established on accountability and graduate follow-up procedures. The Ohio Business Teachers Association (OBTA) encouraged and monitored the growth and development of business education programs. The OBTA was a professional business teachers' organization. It included business education teachers from junior high school through college.

Cooperative Office Education (COE), one of the earliest types of business education, was funded by the *George-Barden Act* and supervised by the T&I education service. Then a federal audit halted the funding of COE until Ohio's General Assembly and the State Board of Education provided state support. In 1957, 13 schools were operating cooperative office education programs at their own expense. With encouragement from the OBTA, the State Board of Education reinstated COE funding in 1958. Vocational Education Director Ralph Howard and Assistant State Superintendent for Public Instruction Dwight Darling were key in supporting this action.

In 1953, the General Assembly had passed a line item to establish a position of supervisor of business education in the Department of Education. However, it was not until 1957 that Robert Balthaser was appointed BOE supervisor in the Division of Vocational Education. One of Balthaser's first acts was to institute a block-time program for business programs.

The block-time programs provided three hours of practice in the skills of the occupational program and 1.5 hours of instruction in related technical information, mathematics, and communications skills—reading, writing, listening, speaking—essential for performing the task/s at hand. Relevant mathematics and English content were borrowed from the academic areas and applied to business education. BOE, was defined as *learning experiences designed to lead to employment*

*or advancement of individuals in occupations in public or private enterprises or orga-
nizations related to a facilitating function of the business office.*

Following passage of the *1963 Vocational Education Act* and Ohio's Joint
Vocational School law, major expansion of business and office education programs began. The growth encouraged leaders to make changes.

While principal at the Warren Local High School, Gordon Eddy set up the
first BOE laboratory with office-size desks and adjustable chairs. Eddy later
became assistant state supervisor for BOE. New laboratories were equipped with
the latest typewriters, closed-system telephone systems, and remote audio equipment to simulate transcription procedures for secretarial training. In later years
personal computers were introduced for teaching word processing, data-based
reporting, and spreadsheets.

Model BOE curricula were developed, and The Ohio State University's BOE
faculty, led by Inez Ray Wells, conducted workshops and published a COE
teacher's manual.

In cooperation with the 3M Corporation, the BOE staff at Bowling Green
State University created a model curriculum—APEX. Drs. James Bowling of
Bowling Green State University, William Jennings of The Ohio State University,
and Lucille Wright of Cleveland State University collaborated in this effort.
Assistant State Supervisor George Bell monitored the process. Dr. Lillian King at
Akron State University developed an interpretative guide for the state BOE curriculum model for new non-degree instructors in programs such as printing and
data processing. Ansonia High School teacher Claire Lynch developed a self-gen-
erated manual for first-year students to construct office simulation activities for
use in the second-year program. The Instructional Materials Laboratory at The
Ohio State University became the instructional resource materials distribution
center for BOE teachers.

Initially, the BOE Service supported only the secretarial training program.
This narrow approach to business education limited student enrollment and was
designed to prepare individuals for only one level of employment in the workforce. The occupation of secretary required proficiency in shorthand and transcription. This required at least an average or above-average ability level on the
part of the student. The BOE service was encouraged to open additional avenues
for youth to enter business occupations. Responding to the challenge, Robert
Francis, a BOE assistant supervisor, developed an offset printing program as one
example of a broader business education curriculum.

After 1963, program offerings were expanded even more over the next several
years. The expanded BOE program offerings included:

Accounting and computing; bank teller; business data processing systems; general office clerical and filing; information communications, materials support, transporting, storing and recording; personnel, training and related occupations; stenographic, secretarial and related occupations; supervisory and administrative occupations; typing and related occupations, and miscellaneous office occupations.

The constant evolution of skill requirements in the work world and the capability of vocational business office education to combine content from various occupational areas demonstrated the value of bringing a number of occupational areas together in JVS districts career centers. These situations allowed an economy of effort and breadth of opportunities. In many cases, busing was needed to bring together the number of students needed for a broad program, one that would give students the choices related to their interests and needs. Legislation in Ohio and the leadership from the individual vocational service areas in the Division of Vocational Education had broadened the opportunities for youth.

Program expansion created a need for youth group activities. Ernestine Kyle at Ravenna High School noted the existing club programs did not encompass the breadth of occupational areas in the field of business and office occupations. Nor did the existing competitive skills program support the breadth of program offerings that had evolved.

In 1966, the Business Professionals of America was formed. It encompassed the full range of vocational business programs in Ohio and other states. The national office, located in Columbus, directed the annual competitive skills events started by Dr. Don Bright of Bowling Green State University and Donald Potter, assistant state BOE supervisor.

Over the years, the number of business and office education programs grew steadily from the original COE programs that were common in smaller schools to laboratory-based BOE programs offered in some small cities and suburbia. But with the advent of the joint vocational school movement across the state, BOE program growth greatly accelerated. Most of the new programs were located in JVS districts and major cities where the program breadth of occupational training was matched by a comparable breadth of employment opportunities. In 1983, enrollment in high school BOE peaked with 2,033 male students and 23,450 female students.

DISTRIBUTIVE EDUCATION AND
OCCUPATIONAL WORK ADJUSTMENT (OWA)
Contributed by Bernard Nye

The use of federal funds for distributive education was authorized at both the state and local levels by the *1936 George-Dean Act* (PL 74-673). Designed as a program of vocational instruction, distributive education was to prepare, maintain and advance people in sales and marketing occupations. Distributive occupations included those for workers engaged in buying, selling, storing, transporting, risk-bearing, financing, standardizing, and grading activities. They involved distributing products and services of farm and industry to consumers, or managing, operating, or conducting retail, wholesale, or service businesses.

Marguerite Loos was appointed state supervisor of distributive education in 1936 and directed it until August 1962. Dr. Bernard Nye then led the program until he retired in August 1983. Upon Nye's retirement, the distributive education and BOE services were combined into business and marketing education.

The state distributive education and OWA staff included four supervisors for high school programs, four adult consultants, one post-secondary supervisor, one materials laboratory consultant, three teacher-educators, one OWA supervisor, and one OWA teacher-educator. All were highly competent individuals, who strongly believed in their roles in program development and improvement. The instructional materials laboratory consultant, with the assistance of private-sector distributive business consultants, developed specialized instructional materials to be used in secondary and adult-level distributive education programs throughout the state.

By 1963, distributive education consisted of secondary school programs and short-term adult programs designed to assist persons already employed in distributive occupations. Approximately 70 secondary programs were in operation and more than 3,000 adults per year were improving their skills and opportunities for occupational advancement.

Advisory committees comprised of local employers and employees assisted the distributive education instructors in developing and promoting distributive education programs throughout Ohio. The committees served as sounding boards for program improvement ideas and class projects.

As the need for training became more evident and training opportunities more available, both secondary and adult distributive education programs grew, especially with the advent of the joint vocational schools. In the late 1960s, the number of secondary programs had doubled to more than 120. The adult programs annually served more than 10,000 enrollees.

During the 1970s, a number of high school distributive education programs were initiated that involved two-year, in-school laboratory experiences for both junior and senior high school students. From the laboratory-based programs, students gained skills and technical understandings, including advertising, hospitality management, retail sales, and similar occupations.

By the late 1970s, there were more than 400 secondary distributive education programs. More than 25,000 adults employed in distribution occupations were being served by instructional programs. Distributive education (now called marketing education) remains a strong component of Ohio's vocational education program.

The need for additional distributive education coordinators and instructors led to the establishment of teacher education centers at The Ohio State, Bowling Green State and Kent State Universities. Prospective distributive education teacher candidates were required to have a strong and successful background in a distributive occupation.

Distributive Education Clubs of America (DECA)

The distributive education state leadership staff noted the significance of youth organizations in the other vocational services and formed a Distributive Education Club in Ohio soon after the in-school programs began. Subsequently, the state club affiliated with the national youth organization for distributive education, the Distributive Education Clubs of America (DECA). As the number of programs grew, the number of students participating in club activities increased. Club activities included civic and community improvement projects, competitive marketing and sales events, social and recreational activities, and professional and personal growth opportunities. One of Ohio DECA's major activities was raising funds for the Special Olympics for disabled youth.

Many Ohio DECA students won valuable prizes and scholarships as a result of their accomplishments in the competitive events held at the national level. Also, a number of Ohio DECA members have been elected to national offices.

In the 1940s, Amanda Thomas became the first DECA state advisor. There are no other records prior to 1967 about other state advisors and their dates of service

OWA

In the early 1970s, through a program entitled occupational work adjustment (OWA), the distributive education service and staff were given opportunities to organize programs for disadvantaged youth, ages 14 and 15. These students were academically challenged in various ways. Because of their inability to achieve academically, they had deemed themselves failures. They were in need of some successes in school and life in general.

The OWA program assigned eligible students to an OWA coordinator, who placed them in paid jobs for not less than two hours a day. OWA students would also spend an additional two periods daily with the OWA coordinator, who would assist them in adjusting to their jobs and improving their basic skills in reading and writing. OWA's goal was to improve the students' sense of self-worth and assist them in succeeding in a job. OWA students could return to a regular academic program at any time. When they reached the 11th grade, they could enroll in either academic or vocational programs.

OWA provided opportunities to experience success, and encouraged program enrollees to stay in school. Nearly 400 OWA programs had been initiated in local school systems.

HOME ECONOMICS (FAMILY AND CONSUMER SCIENCES) EDUCATION
Contributed by Sonia Price

With the passage of the *Smith-Hughes Act* in 1917, home economics education became an integral part of the American educational system. It has been reported that one senator's wife told him as he left the house, *Don't forget the ladies*. The role of the "ladies" was homemaking. The act provided that 20% of the funds authorized for T&I education could be spent for vocational home economics education.

During the early years in Ohio, most federal money was spent on high school programs for 14-year-old girls, or women age 16 and over who wanted to prepare themselves or extend their knowledge related to homemaking responsibilities. A few part-time school programs were organized for women and girls who had little experience as housekeepers. Those programs ran for a minimum of 144 hours a year.

A survey of schools in 1921 revealed that home economics was offered in all but five major cities and in 24 of 31 exempted village schools. Emphasis was also placed on establishing evening adult classes for women as well as cooperating with the American Red Cross in developing lunchroom programs in many schools. Treva E. Kauffman was the first state home economics supervisor. She served from 1918 to 1921.

In 1924, the Bedford High School Home Economics Club applied to the adult American Home Economics Association (AHEA) for membership and was accepted. Many clubs took the name Betty Lampers from the national AHEA symbol. Beryl Cone of Plains High School organized a club in 1930 under the name of Future Homemakers. This resulted in two separate home economics clubs. In 1936, the first state meeting of the Future Homemakers Association (FHA) was held and a constitution was adopted.

In 1943, anticipating that a merger would strengthen the youth organization, AHEA appointed a committee to study high school homemaking programs. A year later, June 1944, AHEA and the Home Economics Education Branch of the U.S. Office of Education became co-sponsors of the organization. The National Education Association and the American Vocational Association became cooperating groups. In 1945, Ohio was granted its official Future Homemakers of America charter.

In 1940, Enid Lunn, the second state home economics supervisor (1921-1958), published the state's course of home economics study for secondary programs. The course of study was built around persistent personal and home living problems of high school students. Subjects included food and nutrition, clothing and related art, home management, home furnishings and housing, and family and other social relationships.

Future Homemakers of America (FHA)

By 1958, Ohio had 390 FHA chapters with 18,224 members. Home economics classes had 31,091 secondary students; another 44,664 people attended adult homemaking classes. Margaret McEniry became Ohio's third state supervisor in 1958 and served until 1969.

In 1962, the year before Congress passed the *Vocational Education Act* to expand vocational education services, Ohio's vocational home economics enrollments totaled 61,307, including 26,973 in secondary education and 34,335 in adult education. There were 17,231 members in 374 FHA chapters.

Related Occupations and Program Expansion

By 1968, enrollment had more than doubled to 132,644, including 103,045 in secondary education and 25,599 in adult education. Growing enrollments reflected not only an increasing population, but the addition of customized programs that better served youths and adults. Federal legislation in 1963, 1968, and 1976 had broadened the scope of vocational education and encouraged expansion of vocational education nationally, including home economics education.

Vocational home economics was a natural adjunct to wage-earning programs. The articulation between family life and work life was crucial to a healthy economy and employment. The missions were complementary. The *1963 Vocational Education Act* led to the writing of a state plan for vocational education, including home economics.

During the 1964-1965 school year, a new curriculum was developed for junior and senior high school programs. Operations manuals for new programs in home economics-related occupations at the secondary and adult levels became a reality. Pilot programs were initiated and secondary and adult enrollments skyrocketed to 86,165. At the adult level, six-hour, job-related courses were offered to provide new skills as well as upgrade existing skills for women employed outside the home. In 1968, two post-secondary technical programs in home economics—food-service management and child development—enrolled 173 students including 20 male students.

By 1968, it was evident the homemaking curriculum needed adjustment. Historically, the primary goal of vocational home economics was preparing youth and adults for the vocation of homemaking and improved family living. But now greater emphasis was being given to management and consumer education. The goal was to help students, male and female, adjust to their dual roles as family members and wage earners.

Impact & Family Life Education

At the same time, two special programs—"impact" and "family life education"—were planned to meet the needs of persons living in economically depressed areas. The "impact" program was designed to keep dropout-prone junior high students in school. State guidelines, curriculum development and in-service offerings for teachers took priority.

The family-life education pilot program was initiated in 1968 in four metropolitan federal housing centers. Participants received assistance in the various aspects of home and family life as well as basic education. Each center had a parent-child interaction program that included child-care facilities. Those programs (sometimes called infant stimulation) provided qualitative experiences for infants and parents.

Because adults living in these centers had extensive needs, joint efforts with other social service agencies were necessary. In Cleveland, the Metropolitan Housing Authority provided free classroom space so that classes could be held where the students lived. The Cuyahoga County Welfare, County Extension Service, Welfare Federation, Central Volunteer Bureau, Neighborhood Youth Corps, Resident Councils, and the Cleveland Public Schools all supported the program.

Occupational programs reached 7,456 secondary students in 1972-73. Ten institutions offered post-secondary technical education. An innovative therapeutic recreational occupation program was initiated in 1975. Full-time gainful employment adult programs grew to 22. Three were designed to serve the disabled and other disadvantaged populations. Adult short-term supplemental and preparatory courses were offered in a majority of the VEPDs.

Social Service Agency Partnering

In 1975, home economics state staff members participated with the Department of Welfare in a project entitled Team Training in Ohio Child Abuse and Neglect. HEW's Office of Child Development funded the project. Selected vocational teachers attended the five-day curriculum sessions. They became the leaders in regional and local in-service meetings for all vocational home economics teachers in the fall of 1977.

In coordination with the Welfare Department, the home economics service also developed 14 child-care curriculum modules for day-care workers. Offered in adult education programs, they were a requirement for the workers' certification. Likewise, curriculum modules were developed for upgrading skills of food-service workers.

Over the years there was an increase in the number of male students in home economics classes. To help teachers meet their gender-equity goals, the home economics service developed *A Male Role Today and Tomorrow* curriculum guide. Impact programs grew to 105. Family-life programs were offered in 12 major city and rural poverty areas. In all, there were 171 centers. The home economics offerings were widely accepted by the poverty-stricken participants.

Twenty-five programs were designed to assist displaced homemakers with skill training, management of home and children, and economic independence. Federal and state Comprehensive Employment Training Act (CETA) funds assisted in the start-up of those programs.

GRADS and GOALS

The home economics state staff was also instrumental in the design of the Graduation, Reality and Dual-Role Skills (GRADS) program to assist pregnant adolescent girls and young parents who were still in school. The focus was on dropout prevention. CETA funds also helped support this program. Its goals were to increase the likelihood that students would remain in school during their pregnancy and graduate, encourage goal-setting directed toward the concept of the dual-role of employee and parent, expose students to the reality of the work world in their local communities, assist participants in carrying out positive health-care practices for themselves and their children in both prenatal and postnatal stages, and provide knowledge and skills related to positive parenting practices.

The program was soon featured in the National Vocational Showcase sponsored by the National Association of State Directors of Vocational Education and the National Council on Vocational Education. In 1989, the GRADS curriculum was revised for nationwide dissemination and many other states implemented the program.

A 1996 Ohio report on GRADS highlighted its effectiveness. There were 10,619 females and 1,372 males enrolled in the program. There were also 11,160 children from age 0 to age 3 served through their parents, including 7,003 female students who were pregnant at some time during the school year. There were 5,201 live births to GRADS students. Another 5,110 students were parenting infants. GRADS teachers served an average of 47 students annually and had made 40,265 home, hospital, and family contacts.

A second CETA-supported home economics initiative was Graduation, Occupational and Living Skills (GOALS). This program served students ages 16 to 21 who were high school dropout single parents in need of a helping hand to encourage them to re-enter a secondary education program customized to their needs. Success for the students meant earning their high school diploma and obtaining full-time employment, or pursuing further skill training.

In 1969, Sonia Cole Price was appointed assistant director of vocational education for vocational home economics in the Ohio Department of Education.

She served in that role through 1982, when she became an associate director in the Division of Vocational Education. Her term of leadership saw increased enrollments at all levels. In December 1983, Price received the Outstanding Service Award from the Vocational Home Economics Division of the American Vocational Association. The Ohio Vocational Association also honored her leadership.

By the end of her term as head of the home economics service, secondary vocational home economics programs were being offered in all 102 VEPDs.

Consumer Economics

The Ohio Department of Education's Home Economics Service also had the responsibility for providing leadership in consumer economics education. In 1971, a state staff person was employed to work in coordination with the Ohio Council on Economic Education in developing economic education curricula and teacher workshops for several academic and vocational areas. Three local coordinators were hired to coordinate consumer education concepts and provide in-service activities to teachers (grades K through adult). By 1980, there were 19 economic education coordinators throughout the state.

Local Supervision

To accommodate the extensive changes in curriculum and other offerings in the early 1970s, VEPDs hired a total of 37 local vocational home economics supervisors to plan, lead and implement new programs. The Division of Vocational Education provided special grants to expand resource centers in local school districts that had hired home economics supervisors. Matching funds were made available for child-care equipment and for household management repair kits. Students could take household repair kits home after class for their personal use. The home economics service also created an educational TV program, *Two-Way Street*, to reinforce class instruction and the service also published a newsletter, *News and Notes*, for teachers.

Special Initiatives

The *1984 Carl D. Perkins Act* once again brought changes to programming. Two main themes prevailed. First, the act sought to make vocational education accessible to all persons, including disabled and disadvantaged persons, single parents and homemakers, adults in need of training and retraining, persons participating in programs designed to eliminate sex bias and stereotyping in vocational education, and incarcerated persons.

Second, the act sought to improve the quality of vocational education programs in order to improve productivity and promote economic growth.

In home economics, grants were provided for single parents and displaced homemakers to promote participation in occupational programs. Funds were provided to support program tuition, child-care expenses, transportation, and support services. The Work and Family Work-site Program was rolled out.

In 1986, a teenage suicide prevention project called *TAP* was developed by FHA leadership and its state officers. *TAP* received much publicity nationally as well as in Ohio. A *Practical Action Curriculum* for secondary teachers was also published and many local in-service meetings were held to assist teachers to use this new teaching approach.

In 1988, the Vocational Home Economics Education Service became the Family and Consumer Sciences Education Service. It had the following objectives:

- To promote knowledge, skills, attitudes, and behaviors to prepare youth and adults for family life, work, and careers in family and consumer sciences.

- To strengthen the well-being of individuals and families across the life span.

- To create responsible citizens and leaders in family, community and work settings.

- To promote optimal nutrition and wellness across the life span.

- To teach students to manage resources to meet the material needs of individuals and families.

- To teach students to balance personal, home, family and work life.

- To teach students to use critical and creative thinking skills to address problems in diverse family, community, and work environments.

- To coach students in creating successful life management, employment and career development.

- To educate students to function effectively as providers and consumers of goods and services.

- To teach students to appreciate human worth and accept responsibility for their actions and success in family and work life.

From its inception to present day, home economics education has been an integral and vital part of the vocational education movement in Ohio and has enjoyed continuous innovation, growth and success.

TRADE AND INDUSTRIAL EDUCATION (T&I), HEALTH CAREERS AND OCCUPATIONAL WORK EXPERIENCE (OWE)
Contributed by Byrl Shoemaker and Harry Davis

The *Smith-Hughes Act of 1917* (PL 347) included T&I education. The first supervisor in Ohio, E.L. Heusch, was appointed in 1918. Only eight persons have held that position. They were Heusch (1917-1945), Robert M. Reese (1945-1956), Byrl Shoemaker (1956-1962), Earl Fowler (1962), Harry Davis (1962-1982), James Wiblin (1982-1997), Robert Bowermeister (1997-2003), and Kathy Sommers (2003-present).

Reese and Lawrence Borsage, his assistant, encouraged the expansion of T&I programs beyond the major cities to all youth. A reasonable amount of expansion for limited program services was achieved in the early and mid-1950s. Diversified programs, using the cooperative education model, placed students in jobs in local industries. Reese and Borsage also initiated limited in-school training programs in smaller cities. But the majority of the students outside the major cities still did not have a broad range of choice.

T&I education leaders in the state supported the experimental area school concept in Pike County. They also supported the passage of the joint vocational school district law (Section 3313.90, Ohio Revised Code). Shoemaker welcomed the opportunities provided by the passage of the 1963 JVS law, envisioning opportunities to provide an expanded program of career and technical education, including T&I education, throughout rural Ohio.

In the early 1960s, enrollments in T&I programs were:

	Enrollment	Trade Areas	Schools	Cities
Secondary T& I (11th and 12th grades)	8,347	32	105	
Pre- Employment Adult programs	2,842	8		36
Supplemental Adult Classes	49,458	32		50
Apprenticeship-related Instruction	6,699	24		31

Only 3% of eligible 11th and 12th grade students were enrolled in T&I classes across the state. The number of adults enrolled did not compare favorably to the fact that 42% of working adults were employed in T&I occupations in Ohio.

The JVS law of 1963 and the 1969 law requiring the formation of vocational planning districts benefited all vocational services. T&I education, however, probably had the most to gain. By the 1967-68 school year, the number of youth and adults served were:

High School	18,000
Adult Preparatory	4,600
Supplementary	55,000
Apprenticeship	10,000
Total	87,600

Among the 18,000 secondary students, 3,700 were classified as special needs.

The 1969 state law requiring the development of vocational planning districts again provided a growth spurt to T&I education throughout the state. By 1971-72, secondary enrollment had doubled and overall enrollments had increased by 26.3% to 109,893.

High School	36,062
Adult Preparatory	8,831
Supplementary	65,000
Apprenticeship	N/A
Total	109,893

From 1962-63 to 1967-68 the following preparatory programs were introduced in those districts where there were matching job opportunities: appliance repair, small engine repair, heating/air-conditioning, building maintenance and custodial services, diesel/truck mechanics, painting and decorating, computer maintenance and repair, chemical laboratory assistant, and aviation frame and power mechanics.

From the 1968-69 to the 1971-72 school year an additional menu of programs were added at one or more vocational centers, including the masonry trades, electrical lineman, mine mechanics, telecommunications, and radio and TV station operation and maintenance. And in the 1972-73 school year more programs were offered, including plumbing, marine maintenance, mineworker, auto service and repair, business machine maintenance, and maritime services.

Program growth motivated by state and federal legislation and the additional state, federal and local funding not only increased the numbers of youth and adults served; it increased the opportunities for training both youth and adults. The scope of the offerings for youth and adults depended on the number of people available for training and available funding.

The special populations served within the numbers reported above and the services to the teachers and administrators of the programs at the local level were an important part of this success story.

Health Occupations—Practical Nursing

The practical nurse training program prepared persons in a one-year program to provide bedside nursing services in support of a registered nurse or doctor. A number of health-service procedures were identified and approved for practical nurse training, and were included in the program's curriculum. The instructional program included classroom instruction, laboratory demonstrations and practice, and clinical experience in a hospital.

In the 1950s, legislation had required a state board test for graduates of practical nurse training programs with the issuance of a license for those who passed the test. Much of the practical nurse training program's curriculum was predicated on preparing students to pass the state board test.

The state director of vocational education assigned responsibility for administering programs in health-related occupations to the T&I Service when a private school in Cleveland and the public schools in Cincinnati launched practical nurse training in 1946-48.

Most of the programs were full-time programs for adults and were offered through technical institutes and community colleges under the direction of the Board of Regents. All of the programs were required to meet the standards of the State Board of Nursing.

There were, however, one or two programs operating at the high school level as a part of the vocational offerings. Those programs were successful in preparing a limited number of youth for this important health occupation field. However, the State Board of Nursing established regulations preventing additional programs at the secondary level, even though practical nurse training programs continued to be in demand.

In 1956, the first full-time staff person for practical nurse training administration was employed in the T&I Service of the Ohio Department Education, Division of Vocational Education.

Dental Assistant Programs

In 1958, the first dental assisting training programs were initiated. Experimental programs in university-based dental colleges indicated that a person trained to provide chair-side assistance to a dentist increased the dentist's productivity. At the secondary level, where most of the dental assisting programs were offered, it was a two-year program.

During the first year, students received all of their instruction in the school-based classroom and laboratory. During the second year, students were in school for a half day and spent the other half day in a dentist's office gaining clinical and practical on-the-job experience. Training programs were also offered at the adult level in both private and public education institutions. National certification was available for students who completed a dental assistant program and met all of the certification requirements.

Medical Assistant and Diversified Health Occupations Programs

In 1969, the first medical assistant training programs began in Columbus and Parma. This program was similar to the dental assisting program in structure and operation. Most programs were offered at the secondary level.

Since some planning districts did not have a sufficient number of students to offer individual programs in dental or medical assisting, diversified health occupation training programs were approved in 1969 and spread across the state. Such programs provided education and training through the cooperative education model. Students received classroom instruction at school and learned their skills on-the-job from a dentist, doctor, or nurse.

Medical Laboratory Assistant

The Montgomery County JVS (now known as the Miami Valley Career Technology Center) started the first medical laboratory assistant program in 1972. The program was designed to prepare persons to assist medical laboratory technicians. Although similar programs were established in other vocational centers, as of 1987 the Montgomery County program was the only one to have achieved national accreditation

Vocational Industrial Clubs of America (VICA/ SkillsUSA)

Early on the vocational service areas of agriculture, home economics and distributive education had youth club organizations. Club programs, which took place after school, provided leadership training opportunities and competitive events at the local, state and national levels. The U. S. Office of Education promoted these club organizations and guided them nationally.

In the early years of T&I education, the T&I Education Service in the U. S. Office of Education promoted the concept of club programs, but was opposed by organized labor. Labor feared such clubs would become a competitive labor organization.

Local supervisors of T&I programs, however, saw value in the youth club programs in other vocational areas. They encouraged the state T&I service to establish a youth program for T&I students. In 1952, the state T&I office convened a meeting to consider a club program. Approximately 25 local supervisors attended. Agricultural education professor Ralph Bender of The Ohio State University spoke in favor of the idea. He cited the benefits received by students in vocational agriculture education. The group voted to establish a club program. State T&I Education Supervisor Reese was named director of the new organization. His assistant, Shoemaker, became the club advisor.

Shoemaker immediately called on the leadership of Ohio's two major labor organizations. He met with the secretary of the American Federation of Labor (AFL) and with a representative of the Congress of Industrial Organizations (CIO). Both labor organizations supported the idea of a youth club for T&I education. Each organization appointed a member to assist in the effort. Shoemaker also met with Lincoln Electric Welding Company vice president A. F. Davis, who volunteered his support.

Forming local clubs was voluntary, but encouraged by the state leadership staff. The clubs grew quickly to almost 4,000 members statewide. An annual state conference sponsored competitive events. The first competitive event was in leadership training, including public speaking and parliamentary procedure. As the clubs grew, other competitive events were added in the occupational skill and knowledge areas.

Vocational Industrial Clubs of Ohio was selected as the organization's name because Texas had the largest club of this type in the nation. When a national youth organization of T&I students was incorporated in1966, Shoemaker correctly anticipated that it would be called the Vocational Industrial Clubs of America. Both the national and state VICA clubs have prospered with the help of T&I teachers and support from organized labor and management. Ohio was one of the founding members of the national VICA organization.

In Ohio, VICA has enjoyed excellent state leadership. Beginning in 1986, Jeff Merickel served tirelessly as Ohio's advisor for VICA. Annually, contest activities used several large buildings at the Ohio Exposition Center to accommodate the state competitive skills events. Thousands of VICA members and their advisors attended the annual state awards banquet in the year 2000. Merickel brought Ohio's VICA program to the forefront in the nation and by the year 2000, Ohio had more than 29,000 VICA members. The next closest state was Pennsylvania with 17,000. The advisors who preceded Merickel were Shoemaker, Carl Schaefer, Merle Strong, Ralph Neal, Charles Dygert, and Robert Whisman.

VICA and its predecessor in Ohio—the Vocational Industrial Club of Ohio (1952-1966)—have provided T&I students with leadership and citizenship experiences, as well as motivational opportunities to compete and excel in the demonstration of skills and knowledge related to their chosen occupational areas. The skill areas included the trades, health occupations and occupational work experiences. The clubs reflected (and still do) a commitment of the teachers to the needs of youth.

PUBLIC SERVICE PROGRAMS

Fire Service Training

Ohio's major cities have always had training programs for their full-time fire service employees. However, most rural areas had fire protection through volunteer fire departments. Smaller fire departments could not afford a full-time chief, much less training for volunteer firefighters. In the 1940s, the T&I service established a training program for volunteers.

The T&I service trained selected volunteer firefighter trainers. They, in turn, trained volunteer firefighters serving fire departments in the smaller, mostly rural and sparsely populated communities around the state. The T&I Instructional Materials Laboratory at The Ohio State University developed the first fire-service training manual in the nation for volunteer firefighters. The program worked well. The service was extended to all volunteer departments in the state. T&I staff members also organized regional weekend fire schools to bring the latest techniques to a broad number of departments. This program continued into the mid-1980s.

Emergency Rescue Training

In 1959, as T& I Supervisor Shoemaker was returning from a meeting in southern Ohio, he observed victims of a highway accident being treated by a volunteer emergency medical team. Upon reaching his office, Shoemaker contacted one of the experienced fire-service training coordinators to ask who trained volunteer emergency rescue squad members. He learned that, although the city squads received training, there was no comparable training for emergency medical volunteer squads.

As a result, the T&I service established training for volunteer emergency medical team members as part of its public-service training program. The emergency medical training program followed the template of the fire-service training program. Qualified emergency rescue service personnel were employed to train part-time instructors. The full-time instructors visited volunteer emergency squad units and assisted them in scheduling a trained instructor for that squad. Through the auspices of T&I programs, the Division of Vocational Education reimbursed part of the instructional costs.

Initially, adequate training information and resources were lacking for instructors and students alike. Employed as one of the emergency rescue training coordinators, Jack Liberator, a registered nurse with extensive experience, had contacts with a number of doctors and other nurses. He developed the first emergency rescue squad training manual. Assisted by colleagues in the health care profession, Liberator prepared a manual that became the bible for rescue squads throughout the nation. The T&I service directed the program until a statewide board was established in the 1980s.

Training in the Corrections Institutions

People incarcerated in Ohio's state prisons needed both social and occupational rehabilitation. With its commitment to serve the needs of the disadvantaged and handicapped, T&I education provided occupational skill-training opportunities to prison inmates. In consultation with the Ohio Department of Rehabilitation and Corrections, T&I found that the greatest need in launching and sustaining such a program was teacher education and educational supervision.

In 1972, T&I employed two individuals to work with the Department of Rehabilitation and Corrections to improve the training programs in state correctional institutions. Both were employed through a contract with the T&I teacher education unit at The Ohio State University.

Neil Johnson was charged with improving the occupational training programs in correctional institution. Theodore Shannon was employed as the corrections program teacher-educator. The Department of Rehabilitation and Corrections was very supportive. The teachers in the correctional institutions became part of the vocational family. They joined the Ohio Vocational Association and had special professional development programs at the OVA annual conference.

Law Enforcement Training

In the early 1960s small police departments did not have any source of organized law enforcement training. The T& I service initiated a training program for law enforcement personnel, following the pattern established for fire service training. Competent law enforcement officers with the necessary experience, technical skills, and knowledge in law enforcement were identified and trained to conduct classes for enforcement officers employed in small police departments.

T&I Teacher Education

T&I education and health occupations had unique challenges in recruiting and preparing teachers of skilled occupations. Normally, it took a minimum of four years of experience as a learner and an additional two years as a journeyman worker for a person to acquire the necessary skills and technical knowledge to prepare youth for employment. Such a pathway to occupational proficiency was not a part of a traditional university-based teacher education program.

The teacher education model designed to prepare T&I teachers was to employ teacher candidates who had a minimum of six years of successful work experience in the trade or occupation, then provide them with the necessary pedagogical skills training. The teacher-education process included four weeks of pre-employment instruction on a full-day basis at an approved teacher education center. That was followed by classroom observation and mentoring by a teacher-educator every two weeks for two years. Instructors also attended a two-week workshop of full-day instruction at the end of the first year of teaching. Under the guidance of the teacher-educator, the instructor completed the teacher education course of study during the second year.

In the early 1940s, the University of Toledo and the University of Akron hosted the teacher education programs under the sponsorship of the two cities. Harry Paine and Charles Felker were the teacher-educators at the University of Toledo. Dallas Downing filled that role in Akron. In the late 1940s, Paine moved to the University of Cincinnati and Felker remained in Toledo. When Felker retired, G. Eric Williams took his place. The teacher education center at Akron moved to Kent State University under the leadership of Ted Steiner. Because of the size of Cleveland City School's T&I program, Cleveland had an on-site, full-time teacher-educator, Joseph Roenigk. The Cleveland-based T&I teachers earned college credit through Kent State University.

A T&I instructional materials laboratory, established at Akron in the early 1940s, moved to The Ohio State University in 1945. A T&I teacher education program was also established at Ohio State in 1951 under the leadership of Dr. Joe Strobel.

By 1983, when the goal of an adequate program of vocational education for all students in the state had been realized, Wright State University in Dayton had added a teacher education center. Kent State University had the largest teacher education center primarily because northeastern Ohio had experienced the greatest growth in T&I programs. The instructional materials laboratory and public-service programs were based at The Ohio State University.

Achievement Testing

The T&I service initiated statewide achievement testing in 1953. The first testing involved the skills and technical knowledge for students enrolled in machine trades programs. There were more of these programs in the state than any other trade program. The Ohio State University's T&I Instructional Materials Laboratory led the test development process. Machine-trade teachers and incumbent craftsmen from the industry formed a committee that, based on an occupational analysis, wrote and validated the test questions.

It was not the goal of the achievement testing endeavor to select the outstanding program or students, but to improve instruction. Students could, however, include their test results on their resumes.

Most test questions were multiple choice, but there were a few matching items. Since mechanical and academic learning abilities varied both within a class and between classes, and in different locales throughout the state, the committee decided to use a short form of the California Test of Mechanical and Mental Maturity as an integral part of the testing effort.

Shoemaker recalled the importance of this system during a review of test results for a machine trades class in a northwest Ohio school district. As the superintendent of that district compared the achievement scores of his students with those across the state, he noted that his students rated very low. *In anger,* Shoemaker recalled, *he said he was going to fire the teacher! I told him; Before you fire the teacher you had better review the ability levels of the students. He did that and relented.* The California Test results revealed that his students scored significantly below the state average on mental maturity.

In the late 1950s, additional tests were developed and validated to measure the achievement levels of students in other trade areas. A computer program was written to score the tests, summarize the results, and prepare reports for each program in each school. The summary report for each school provided the achievement score for individual students on each major section of the test, including the California Test. Class averages were given for all parts of the test as well as statewide normative data on student achievement.

The same tests were given both years in the two-year program to measure learning gain from year one to year two. The test results were reviewed at the state level to determine whether student growth was being achieved in the second year. When analysis of the electrical trades program test results indicated only slight growth in learning in nearly all programs across the state, the curriculum was evaluated and changes were made in program content. That improved learning outcomes in the second year of the program.

In 1962, all the other job-training services (agriculture, business and office, distributive education) began the same type of tests. Home economics was also included because it had responsibility for occupational training. The instructional materials laboratories developed tests for each area. Ray Rinderer, who headed the T&I laboratory at that time, coordinated the testing effort through the 1970s. By 1982, six states were using the Ohio achievement tests and its test evaluation services. More than 80,000 tests were distributed and processed annually for programs in Ohio.

No history of T&I would be complete without identifying those who served as area supervisors during the great growth period. Those able and respected professionals were Philip Anderson, Eric Williams, Thomas McConnaughy, Jack Volkmer, and Thomas Hyde.

8

Career and Technical Teacher Education in Ohio

◆

A Historical Prospective: 1920-2000

by G. James Pinchak

The growth of vocational education has been linked with the development of teacher education and preparation programs in operation in Ohio's universities. Under Ohio law, elementary and secondary teachers must be certificated or licensed in their teaching area(s).

Vocational teacher preparation has been accomplished through one of the two types of programs. Most teachers in Agricultural Education, Business Education, Marketing Education, and Home Economics have come from traditional undergraduate teacher education programs, known in recent years as the Route A program.

Many of the Agricultural Education teachers, and most the Health Occupations teachers, T&I teachers, and more recently Information Technology teachers have been prepared through the Route B program. Historically, the Route B teachers were recruited directly from business and industry. They were hired on the basis of their work experience. They completed their pedagogy education while being employed as a career and technical education teacher and being enrolled concurrently in a university-based teacher education program.

According to Shoemaker, Route B teacher education positions were supported 50% from funds under the *Smith-Hughes Act* beginning in the 1920s at the University of Akron, the University of Cincinnati, The Ohio State University, and the University of Toledo. The original teacher education programs consisted of classroom visitations and seminars on campus spread over a four-year period.

In the 1950s, the Route B structure was changed to add a six-week summer workshop for new teachers and a two-week workshop for second-year teachers in addition to the visitations and seminars. With the addition of the workshops, the program was shortened to two years. Teachers were expected to write a course of study for their program by the end of the second year. Ohio Department of Education, Division of Vocational Education staff assisted in teaching the summer workshops.

Unfortunately, the practices of writing of courses of study fell out of favor in the early 1980s as responsibility for course of study development shifted to the local school districts. School districts were expected to pay teachers supplemental contracts to create courses of study under collective bargaining agreements. Schools elected to use a variety of formats for course of study design. This made it impossible for the Ohio Department of Education or universities to standardize a statewide format.

Shoemaker indicated that the practice of reimbursing teacher education positions at the 50% rate worked well during his tenure and the universities were pleased with the arrangement. The arrangement was particularly critical for T&I education where 100% of the teachers were trained through the industry-based Route B teacher education programs.

In the 1960s, teacher education blossomed as the result of funding through the *Vocational Education Act of 1963* and the *Vocational Amendments of 1968*. In the 1970s, the Ohio Department of Education added some 100% reimbursed teacher education positions for special situations such as Special Needs, Occupational Work Adjustment, and Occupational Work Experience at selected institutions including Bowling Green State University, Cleveland State University, Kent State University, and The Ohio State University.

Dr. A.J. Miller, former chairman of the Department of Vocational Education in the College of Education at The Ohio State University, reported that the high staffing point in his department was in 1975. At that time the department included five non-tenured track positions reimbursed 100% by the Ohio Department of Education, three tenured faculty positions reimbursed at the rate of 50%, and four faculty positions which received no external funding. The college housed three full-time staff members who directed training for firefighters and emergency medical technicians. The department also received funding for eight clerical positions.

According to Miller, the position reimbursement system did not always work smoothly even during the golden era circa 1975. The state reimbursed 50%, but wanted to determine 100% of the staff's activities. Likewise, individuals on a tenure track found it extremely difficult to visit teachers in the field on a regular basis and still meet the university requirements for publishing, research, and service.

In contrast, in 2002 the College of Education at The Ohio State University had one full-time university-supported tenure track position and one non-tenured position funded 100% from an Ohio Department of Education capacity building grant. The university requirement to "publish or perish" was no less intense in the 21st century than it was during the golden age cited by Miller.

The state plan amendments for Ohio in the 1986-87 fiscal year included a teacher education directory that listed funded and non-funded vocational teacher educators in 1985. The number of teacher educators totaled 66 of whom only 47 were funded by the Ohio Department of Education. The distribution of all teacher educators is shown in Table 1. The distribution for funded teacher educators is shown in Table 2. Many of the teacher education positions for traditional baccalaureate programs existed without Ohio Department of Education funding, but the programs addressing teachers recruited directly from business and industry (Route B) were all funded by the Ohio Department of Education.

The funding mechanism for vocational teacher education in Ohio changed in the late 1980s. The Ohio Department of Education *Comprehensive Annual Performance Report* to the U.S. Department of Education, Office of Vocational and Adult Education, stated the following information:

> *Five Vocational Education Regional Personnel Development Centers were created in FY87 (1986-1987), culminating a three-year effort to reform and update teacher education for the 1990s and beyond. Discussion for conversion to a regional personnel development center began in FY84. The National Center for Research in Vocational Education was commissioned to conduct a vocational education teachers' in-service training needs assessment which was completed in April 1986.*
>
> *Numerous factors brought about changes in the linkage pattern of Ohio's vocational teacher education providers and the Ohio Department of Education. These factors included (1) the narrowing federal agenda for vocational education support, (2) the need for teacher education reform, (3) concerns regarding the accessibility of services to teachers in some geographic regions, and (4) the increased need for educational accountability.*
>
> *To address these and other concerns, the division moved from the funding of vocational teacher education via salary subsidies entitlement grants to a system of performance-based contracts awarded to five regional centers. These five regional development centers in Ohio were created to "(1) train new teachers recruited from business and industry, (2) provide in-service training and upgrading for all existing vocational educators, and (3) conduct research."*

For all intents and purposes Ohio Department of Education funding support for undergraduate teacher education programs (Route A) ended in July 1986. The five regional centers that won the competitive grants were:

Northeast Region	Kent State University
Southeast Region	Ohio University
Central Region	The Ohio State University
Southwest	The Ohio State University (Wright State University received the grant in 1990)
Northwest	Bowling Green State University in a consortium with University of Toledo

The in-service activities selected as priorities at the regional centers for the 1987-88 school year were:

1. Motivation of students

2. Techniques and practices for teaching problem solving and decision-making

3. Strengthening vocational education/business-industry relations

4. Expanding time on task for improving classrooms and laboratory management and organizational skills

The grants to Ohio's five regional personnel development centers totaled $1,729,610 in fiscal year 1995.

Division director Parks reported another economic reason for eliminating the staff reimbursement system. Many Ohio universities instituted early retirement buyout offers to reduce the number of top-of-the-pay-scale faculty members. The buyouts of the teacher educators, support staff, and Ohio Department of Education consultant staff on university contacts cost the Ohio Department of Education $3 million in one year alone. Parks said, *The early retirement buyouts were breaking the bank.*

The move to contracting for services instead of positions eliminated the added costs of these buyouts. Furthermore, the State Board of Education wanted the Department of Education to move to competitive-based contracts. The move to contracted services, begun in 1987, appears to have been a permanent change. The position reimbursement is unlikely to return.

Parks stated that universities had also benefited greatly under the *1976 Vocational Education Amendments* because they received two additional types of *Educational Professional Development Act* (EPDA) funds. The funds under section 553 went to the State Department of Education, which then funded professional development projects in the teacher education institutions. Section 552 funds went directly to the universities to fund professional development projects and graduate assistantships.

Federal vocational education legislation after 1976 continued to erode the amounts of federal funds that could be used to fund state leadership activities through the state to the universities and gave increasingly larger shares of the those funds directly to the local school districts.

As the new millennium approached, the Regional Personnel Development Center grants were replaced by Capacity Building Grants to Ohio universities operating both Route A and Route B career and technical education teacher education programs.

Licensure changes throughout the period 1990-2003 shifted the burden for professional development away from universities and school districts and placed the responsibility with individual teachers. Licensure requirements eliminated permanent credentials and required educators to complete more professional development options to meet the requirements for 18 approved Continuing Education Units (CEUs) every five years. Teachers could take structured college courses, but they could also use other professional development activities such as attending pre-approved conferences and seminars, writing curriculum, and participating in local in-service activities to meet the professional development requirements for licensure. By the turn of the century, university coursework was only one of the vehicles for earning CEU equivalents and school districts provided a wealth of opportunities for their employees to earn CEUs without leaving the school district or building.

Vocational teachers hired after 2001 were expected to demonstrate mastery of skills through college course work and performance on the standardized Principles of Learning and Teaching Assessment, known as Praxis II, and in the classroom during the Praxis III assessment process. To meet the myriad of requirements, the programs were once again four years in length, as they were prior to the 1950s.

Technological changes such as email, the internet, high speed modems, broad band communications, and web casts have made it possible for teachers to access vast amounts of information at the stroke of a computer key 24 hours a day, seven days a week. Teacher education no longer needed to be offered synchronously with everyone learning at the same time. Teacher education could now be offered at times convenient to the instructor and students.

The history of vocational teacher education in Ohio offers the following conclusions:

1. The Ohio Department of Education, Division of Vocational Education has given federal funds to Ohio universities for the support of Route B type programs continuously since the 1920s.

2. Ohio Department of Education, Division of Vocational Education funding of traditional vocational education undergraduate programs was eliminated in 1986.

3. External funding from the Ohio Department of Education, Division of Vocational Education was an important motivator for universities to offer and improve teacher education programs.

4. The in-service preparation of Career and Technical educators, particularly Route B programs, has been, and probably will continue to be, viewed by critics in higher education and other areas of teacher education as being outside the traditional teacher education models.

5. These programs must change quickly to respond to changes in state and federal legislation, teacher education standards, new technology and revisions in the academic core of the modern American high school.

Table 1
Numbers of Ohio Vocational Teacher Educators
Listed in the Ohio State Accountability Report for 1985

University	Agricultural Education	Business Education	Marketing Education	Home Economics	Trade & Industry	OWA OWE Special Needs
Akron		1		1		
Ashland				1		
BGSU		1	1	2		
Cincinnati		1			1	
Cleveland State					2	
Kent State	1	2	1	2	7	2
Miami				2		
Mount St. Joseph				1		
Ohio State	11	2	1	6	6	1
Ohio				2		
Toledo					4	
Wilmington	1					
Youngstown				2		
Total	13	7	3	19	20	3

Table 2
Numbers of Funded Ohio Vocational Teacher Educators
Listed in the Ohio State Accountability Report for 1985

University	Agricultural	Business	Marketing	Home Economics	Trade & Industry	OWA/OWE Special Needs
Akron		1				
Ashland						
BGSU		1	1	1		
Cincinnati		1			1	
Cleveland State					2	
Kent State	1	2	1	1	7	2
Miami				1		
Mt. St. Joseph						
Ohio State	4	2	1	4	5	1
Ohio				1		
Toledo					4	
Wilmington	1					
Youngstown				1		
Total	6	7	3	9	19	3

9

Vocational Education for Adults

Adult education played an important role in Ohio's vocational education movement. Since the very early efforts to train skilled craftsmen to meet the employment needs of the state's growing manufacturing economy, through the war production years in the 1940s, up to the present, adult vocational education has grown steadily, both in numbers and in its contributions to an ever-changing social order and work environment.

Adult education probably got its formal beginning with the passage of the *Morrill Act* in 1862. That federal act not only established the land grant college system, it also gave credibility to vocational education. However, it took 55 years from the establishment of land grant colleges for the vocational movement to gain sufficient momentum to achieve the passage of federal legislation regarding the inclusion of vocational education in the public schools. In 1906, several interest groups collaboratively founded the National Society of Industrial Education. This eventually led to the passage of the 1917 *Smith-Hughes Act*. That act specifically referred to vocational education for adults outside the context of a college system.

The *Smith-Hughes Act* provided a vital link that led to a vast array of programs and services available through Ohio's adult vocational education program. Although national data are sketchy, adult vocational education programs and services expanded rapidly after World War I, and reflected the needs of the local workforce and the interests of the participants.

The *1963 Vocational Education Act* was the second most significant piece of federal legislation for adult vocational education. That act stated:

> *It is the purpose of this part to authorize Federal grants to States to assist them to maintain, extend and improve existing programs of vocational education, to develop new programs of vocational education, and to provide part-time employment for youths who need the earnings from such employment to continue their vocational training on a full-time basis, so that persons of all ages in all communi-*

ties of the state—those in high school, those who have completed or discontinued their formal education and are preparing to enter the labor market, those who have already entered the labor market but need to upgrade their skills or learn new ones, and those with special educational handicaps—will have ready access to vocational training or retraining which is of high quality, which is realistic in the light of actual or anticipated opportunities for gainful employment, and which is suited to their needs, interests, and ability to benefit from such training. (Public Law 88-210, 88th Congress, H.R. 4955, December 18, 1963)

Further, the law required that a minimum of one third of the grant had to be spent on those who had completed or left high school for further education, or for the construction of area vocational education facilities, or both. That was significant to Ohio because it provided the opportunity to include adult vocational education in the joint vocational school movement.

While adult vocational education was born and grew modestly prior to 1963, it was greatly enhanced with the passage of the *1963 Vocational Education Act* and the *1968 Vocational Education Amendments*. In the mid-1960s, the State Board of Education adopted the concept that technical education should occur between vocational and professional education. Essentially, the board controlled "technical education" and Ohio's technical colleges were established in 1967 under the auspices of the board and adult vocational education. Although technical education (two-year degree options) was eventually transferred to the Board of Regents, the fact remains that adult vocational education had become a very prominent player in sustaining the productivity of Ohio's workforce.

After the transfer of technical education to the Board of Regents, a "1967 Memorandum of Agreement" was developed between the Regents and the State Board of Education, clarifying the responsibilities of both entities in the area of adult vocational and technical education. The Board of Regents was responsible for the two-year associate degree-granting program and the State Board of Education was responsible for all post-secondary, non-degree adult vocational and technical education. This memorandum served both boards well. It was reconfirmed by joint study commissions in 1983 and again in 1990.

APPRENTICESHIP TRAINING

Apprenticeship is one of the oldest organized patterns of vocational training. An employer trained the student in the occupational skills. The vocational program provided a minimum instruction of four hours weekly in the related mathematics, science, and technical information. The *1917 Smith-Hughes Vocational Education Act* provided for funding apprenticeship classes for out-of-school youth and adults. The program was administered by an apprenticeship training committee. Apprenticeship training committee members included representatives from both management and employees from the respective skilled trades (normally a union representative), or union representatives only.

A written agreement identified the responsibilities of the trainee and the apprenticeship program sponsor. All training agreements for skilled trades required classroom or laboratory instruction to provide the apprentice with the mathematics, science and technical information required to become a knowledgeable and skilled worker in the respective occupation. The T&I education service in the Division of Vocational Education had responsibility for the related training. It was a major function of public vocational education to provide such apprenticeship instruction. However, in some instances, two-year technical institutes or community colleges provided the related academic instruction for apprenticeship training programs.

Most apprenticeship programs existed in the cities where industrial plants had located in earlier years. Often organized labor unions representing the skilled trades played a major role, particularly in the building trades. Until recent years, apprenticeship programs were a major part of the vocational offerings in Canton, Cleveland, Dayton, Sandusky, Toledo, and Youngstown. More recently, business and industry have significantly reduced their apprenticeship programs. Companies were no longer willing to invest in that kind of training.

UPGRADE OR EXTENSION TRAINING

In Ohio, training to upgrade workers' skills attracted the largest enrollments of adults to public vocational education programs. Along with the decline in demand for unskilled labor, the rate of change in existing jobs accelerated and increased the demand for additional training by incumbent workers. There was no set number of hours, days, weeks or years for such training classes. When the desired knowledge or skill level required a longer period of instruction, content was segmented into several sequential components.

Classes were normally offered one or two evenings a week, but they could be taught any time of the day or night for any number of hours. Sometimes the instruction was offered at the business site. Training classes usually included workers from various places of employment, but instruction could be customized for a specialized need of a single employer or union.

Normally, instructors for adult training classes came from the faculty at the vocational center, but persons with demonstrated expertise from a local business or industry could be temporarily certificated to teach. Thus the faculty for a vocational center could include a much larger number of persons than just fulltime faculty employees.

When educational facilities were being constructed or remodeled to accommodate the rapidly growing training needs of new and/or expanding businesses in the community, qualified persons from local business and industrial establishments were used as instructors. The training of 2,000 General Motors workers in Dayton was an example of that type of training flexibility.

PRE-EMPLOYMENT TRAINING

As the number and scope of training facilities grew, the number of pre-employment training programs increased. They met the needs of people who had not been trained for a job or had lost a job and needed to get new or transferable skills for initial entry or re-entry into the workforce.

Changing to new types of employment required trainees to participate in more lengthy and intensive periods of preparation. Instruction and training were normally given on a daily basis so the trainees could become employable as quickly as possible. Before the establishment of joint vocational schools, adult pre-employment training was limited to the major city sites. However, with the advent of the joint vocational centers, as well as vocational centers in other vocational education planning districts, a comprehensive program of adult vocational training was available throughout the state.

Pre-employment training was particularly important when an industry closed and its employees had to seek new types of work. In some cases, college graduates participated in pre-employment training when they were not successful in getting work in their degree specialty. Training was available in the business, T&I, marketing, agriculture, or health-occupation fields. There was no minimum or maximum number of hours established for pre-employment classes. As with upgrading courses, instructors came from the vocational program faculty or from local businesses. This staffing policy made possible instructional program offerings beyond those available within the in-school program. Offerings could, and frequently did, change every year based upon the employment and training needs in the community. All the vocational services provided pre-employment training for adults as the need dictated.

INDUSTRY SPECIFIC TRAINING

A new business or industry, or an existing one that was expanding or changing its operations, often had immediate and unique training needs. Adult vocational programs were developed to meet such needs. Training could be provided at the vocational program site, at the work site, or elsewhere in the community.

As an example, an industry in Marion received a contract that required additional welders. The company asked the Ohio Bureau of Employment Services (OBES)—now part of the Department of Job and Family Services—to import 50 welders from South Korea. OBES contacted the Division of Vocational Education regarding the availability of training assistance.

The Division of Vocational Education staff recommended retraining workers from the Marion area. Since public vocational education facilities in Marion were fully utilized, the division recommended that the company rent a shop facility. The division secured the required welding equipment. Welding instructors were employed from the company as well as from other sources. The division designed the curriculum to the company's specifications. As a result, unemployed people from Marion found new employment.

HOME ECONOMICS FAMILY-LIFE PROGRAMS

Home and family welfare required the contributions of a wage earner. But parenting, nutrition, management, consuming, and homemaking skills were equally critical. The vocational home economics service area in the Division of Vocational Education provided for teaching adults those skills. Prior to the existence of joint vocational schools and other vocational planning districts, vocational home economics programs were offered mostly in the rural areas with an emphasis on homemaking skills. Later the program began to emphasize the other goals of home economics. Major cities, with their unique poverty areas and housing project families, had a ready-made adult clientele for family life programs of instruction.

BUSINESS/INDUSTRY COORDINATION

While vocational education services for adults were available over the entire state, Shoemaker found that information about these services was not always effectively communicated to business leaders. With the assistance of Governor Rhodes and his development director, Shoemaker set up a network of 23 business-industry coordinators.

Shoemaker said the idea for the network came from a visit he made to a plant in northwestern Ohio. As the major employer in a small city, the plant was the mainstay of the local economy. *The plant manager dropped a bombshell,* recalled Shoemaker.

> *He indicated the home company was planning to close the plant because it was not getting enough production. In discussing the problem, I learned the problem was that the employees needed training. I told him there was a joint vocational school nearby, and asked if it could help with his training problem. He said yes. We made arrangements to provide the employees with the needed training. The plant stayed in operation and its people stayed employed.*
>
> *Still, I was frustrated. The vocational center had facilities and instructional services. Several supervisors from the plant served on the center's advisory committees. Yet the plant manager did not know about the available services. Information was not flowing from lower levels of management to top management.*

Shoemaker contacted the state development director. They worked together to create a statewide system of business, industry and education (BIE) coordinators. The chambers of commerce in the largest cities near vocational centers housed the BIE coordinators. The chambers provided the office space and limited office assistance. Vocational funds paid for the coordinators' salaries and travel expenses. The coordinators' responsibility was to get acquainted with industrial and business leaders in their respective communities and then link employment needs for training with available vocational education services.

> *It worked even better than expected,* said Shoemaker.
>
> *Through their relationships with the chambers of commerce, the coordinators were able to make contacts with the top levels of management, assess their training needs, and broker those needs to the appropriate vocational education services in the community. Beyond that, the coordinators became familiar with business and industry needs for information and innovation. They would scour the state for sources that could be brought to the area or link business and industry representatives to other sources in the state.*

In its first year, the business-industry coordination effort served 20,030 adults. Charles Dygert, who had been a tool and die maker and also served as advisor to the Ohio Chapter of the Vocational Industrial Club of America, directed the program. The Vocational Education Division gave him his own budget for training projects. This service was discontinued in the mid-1980s with the appointment of a new development director.

FULL-SERVICE CENTERS

As the joint vocational school movement gained momentum from the 1960s through the mid-1970s, adult education was a required offering in every new center. But there were no specific standards for adult programs or services that were to be offered.

Vocational programs and services varied considerably from community to community. In some instances, the relevancy of such programs was questionable in terms of serving workforce needs. Some districts chose to accommodate only token programs. Others offered a full array from part-time and evening classes to full-time offerings and customized services. There was an apparent need for minimum standards for adult vocational programs and services offered in the various centers.

In 1987, division Director Darrell Parks commissioned Thomas Applegate to develop a new concept of adult vocational education in Ohio; a concept that would efficiently and effectively accommodate Ohio's worker training needs, and provide a complete menu of adult worker support services. Subsequently, the division introduced its Adult Vocational Education Full-Service Center concept via a publication entitled *The Workforce Resource*. Full-service centers quickly gained acceptance across the state and received national recognition. The centers were one-stop shops, providing comprehensive student support services in addition to occupational and technical skill training.

Initially, 32 adult full-service centers were established. They offered the finest in innovative work-force training for employers and employees. Each center had state-of-the-art technology and equipment, experienced instructors, and offered customized programming to meet the diverse job-related and human resource development requirements of business communities that varied in size and specialization.

Support services in each center included adult literacy training, career planning and placement, career transition assistance, child-care services, employee enrichment opportunities, English as a second language, financial assistance, and general educational development (GED) testing.

Testimonials were abundant. Human resources managers from some of Ohio's major corporate entities shared statements like:

- *The training has had a very positive impact on our employees.*

- *We selected the center for its adaptability in programming and in scheduling of training sessions. Our objective is to show quantum improvements in people's productivity.*

- *We had a nice marriage with the Full-Service Center. Our employees gave its instructors high marks.*

State monies were made available annually to the full service centers as performance-based quality enhancement grants. These grants were to help centers sustain a high level of programs and activities. By 1997, 39 adult education facilities had met the criteria to become Full-Service Centers. That year, Ohio's adult education program met the job-related training and retraining needs of approximately 350,000 adults.

In addition to targeted training options and extensive customized training services, adult education had a full-time consultative staff to offer specialized services, such as American College Testing (ACT) Work Keys, ACT Job Profiling, and job-readiness training services. The combination of these strategies established the adult full-service centers as highly effective workforce development allies of business and industry.

Another dimension of the adult vocational education program was its partnership with the One-Stop Career Center System administered by the Ohio Bureau of Employment Services. One-Stop Career Centers offered comprehensive services that were locally designed, with access to Ohio's Job Net, the nation's most advanced job-matching system. The centers' goal was to help link employers and job seekers and to assist both in navigating the maze of service providers available to each. As partners in the One-Stop system, public awareness of Ohio's adult education full service centers was greatly enhanced.

Beginning in 1955 and through 1995, enrollments in adult vocational education programs grew steadily from totals of 60,370 to 225,566, an increase of 274 percent. Part-time adult enrollment peaked in 1982-83 at 289,525, while full-time adult enrollment reached a high of 78,743 in 1989-90. Vocationally funded associate degree and apprenticeship programs accounted for the balance of adult vocational education participants.

10

Education for Career Choice

By 1969 enrollments in vocational education were increasing significantly. It seemed likely the goal of having an adequate program to serve approximately 40% of students in the last two years of high school would be achieved. The Division of Vocational Education then became concerned about assisting young people to make appropriate choices. The division allocated federal funds to design a program to assist students in making informed decisions regarding their future, whether students opted to prepare for work through vocational education programs, or for a profession through a college or university. The new effort was referred to as career education.

Career education, or more accurately education for career choice, was a program that endeavored, through the regular curriculum, to provide all public school youths with motivation to participate in the world of work, to orient them to the many job opportunities available, and to encourage them to actually explore occupations consistent with their respective interests and abilities. The purpose was to enable students to prepare for the world of work. A total career education program includes pre-professional preparation leading to professional training at a college or university, or vocational/technical education leading to successful entry into and advancement in technical occupations. Career education also encouraged youth to take advantage of retraining and upgrading instruction throughout their working life. The concept of life-long education was consistent with changing technology in the world of work as well as the evolution of individual interests and needs.

A total career education program, of which education for choice is a part, included the following:

1. A total *family life program* within the school curriculum. This program emphasized assisting disadvantaged families in the care and motivation of pre-school children, and to create a positive impact on the home life on school-age children.

2. An in-school *career motivation program* for all youth in kindergarten through the sixth grade. The goal was to develop a positive attitude toward the world of work, inspire respect for all work, and create a personal desire to be a part of the world of work.

3. A *career orientation program* in grades seven and eight. This program provided all youth the opportunity to become aware of the many occupations open to those who prepare for them.

4. A *career exploration program* in grades nine and 10, or ages 14 and 15. The goal was to provide all youth the opportunity to examine and gain first-hand experience in several career fields commensurate with individual interests and abilities.

5. A *career preparation program* for youth age 16 and above. It included a comprehensive vocational/technical education program that taught job skills and technical knowledge, as well as the development of desirable work habits and attitudes as a dimension of preparing for employment. The program also offered a comprehensive pre-professional education program that provided knowledge and foundation skills in preparation for professional education beyond high school.

6. A *career training, retraining, and upgrading program* for out-of-school youth and adults. This offered the opportunity throughout adulthood to train, retrain, and upgrade skills, and adjust to technological and societal changes, as well as individual interests and needs.

On the following two pages are reproduced the Ohio Career Development Continuum created to implement the total career education program.

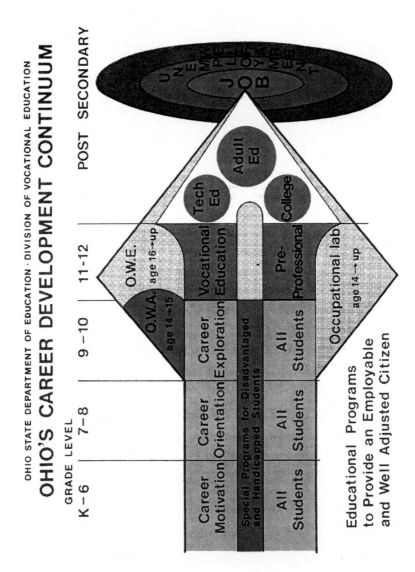

OHIO STATE DEPARTMENT OF EDUCATION · DIVISION OF VOCATIONAL EDUCATION

OHIO'S CAREER DEVELOPMENT CONTINUUM

GRADE LEVEL

K-6   7-8   9-10   11-12   POST SECONDARY

Career Motivation

Career Orientation

Career Exploration

Vocational Education

Special Programs for Disadvantaged and Handicapped Students

O.W.E. age 16-up

O.W.A. age 14-15

Pre-Professional

Occupational lab age 14-up

All Students

All Students

All Students

Adult Ed

Tech Ed

College

UNEMPLOYMENT

JOB

Educational Programs to Provide an Employable and Well Adjusted Citizen

5143

CAREER EDUCATION IN OHIO

Career education is a continuum in education that provides experiences to help individuals make wise career choices, prepare for employment and extend career development throughout life. Career education for choice seeks, through the curriculum, to help all youth build positive self-concepts, become motivated toward the world of work, receive an orientation to the many job opportunities available, and explore several occupations consistent with individual interests and abilities in order to help youth better plan for and benefit from pre-professional or vocational education. The preparation for employment component of career education provides for pre-professional instruction leading to further education and vocational education, technical education, and professional education leading to successful entry and advancement in an occupation of personal choice. Career education through life provides for training, retraining and upgrading instruction throughout an individual's life which is consistent with the technology of the world of work and the individual interests and needs of out-of-school youth and adults.

The successful career education program combines the efforts of the home, school, and community to prepare youth for successful entry into the world of work. A total career education program consists of the following phases:

1. A total *Family Life Program* within the school curriculum with special emphasis for disadvantaged people to help improve the care and motivation of pre-school children and assure a more positive impact of the home on the needs of school age youth.

2. A *Career Motivation Program* for all youth in kindergarten through Grade Six which develops a positive attitude toward the world of work, inspires respect for all work and creates a desire to be a part of the world of work.

3. A *Career Orientation Program* in Grades seven and eight which provides all youth the opportunity to become aware of the many occupations open to those who prepare for them.

4. A *Career Exploration Program* in Grades nine and ten, or age fourteen and fifteen, which provides all youth with the opportunity to examine and gain firsthand experiences with several career opportunities consistent with individual interests and abilities.

5. An *Occupational Work Adjustment (OWA)* for drop-out prone fourteen and fifteen year olds which uses work as an adjustment process to prove to them they are worth something and to encourage them to stay in school and make wise choices of a vocational program at age sixteen.

6. A *Career Preparation Program* for youth age sixteen and above which includes:

    A. a comprehensive vocational education program at the secondary and post-secondary levels which provides job skills and technical knowledge and develops work habits and attitudes in preparation for employment in semi-skilled and skilled occupations.

    B. a comprehensive pre-professional education program which provides knowledge and foundations in preparation for professional education beyond high school.

    C. an *Occupational Work Experience (OWE)* for drop-out prone boys and girls sixteen years of age and older to prepare them for employment through a cooperative type program.

    D. a post-secondary technical education program which provides technical knowledge and experiences in preparation for employment in para-professional occupations.

    E. a professional education program which provides the knowledge and experiences for employment in the professions.

7. A *Career Training, Retraining and Upgrading Program* for out-of-school youth and adults which provides the opportunity throughout adulthood to train, retrain and upgrade skills as technology changes and societal and individual needs and desires dictate.

The career education program was an integral part of the total curriculum and was taught by the regular classroom teachers. External resource experts from various fields of work could be brought into the classroom to supplement the career education content and instructional process. The curriculum design started with identifying the goal and then developing the delivery plan and content based on accepted child development theory and knowledge.

At the elementary level, the emphasis was on *motivation*; work was the focus. The goal was to build a concept of work around factors affecting the lives of the children. Instruction related to the external forces and factors with which the elementary curriculum normally dealt, such as housing, fire and law protection, food, clothing etc. The question was not "what do you want to be?" The goal was to encourage children to contribute to life through some type of work.

The *orientation* function at the seventh and eighth grades was focused on 15 major job families, including professional, technical, skilled and semi-skilled occupations. Through individual subject matter content and practical arts offerings, major job families were identified and appropriate sources of occupational information were researched. Career development coordinators were employed to assist teachers in obtaining appropriate materials and planning relevant field trips.

The *exploration* function at the ninth and 10th grade levels was to provide the young person with career exploration opportunities through practical arts programs in the school or through subject matter classes related to career interests. Visitations to work sites and observations of actual work and the workers were encouraged. The goal was to enable students to make an informed choice regarding future occupations so they could make the best use of their last two years of high school.

Leadership for the K-6 *career motivation* program was assigned to Home Economics Service Supervisor Mabell Black. She encouraged local district administrators to embrace the new program.

With the assistance of Department of Education Director of Guidance John Odgers, his staff and teacher committees developed a teacher manual for the *career motivation* program. The manual set forth goals related to child development levels and suggested activities and strategies to reach the goals. Black often made presentations to groups of educators concerning the total career development program. Karen Heath from the Vocational Home Economics Service assisted Black and later assumed leadership for the entire career education program.

Resource specialists, who were brought into the class for career motivation purposes, were not to encourage youth to choose a specific occupation. They were to explain the importance of work in the lives of the children. The goal was for the children to see work as a social and economic concept and how the work of others affected their lives.

Richard Macer, Special Needs Service assistant director, directed the *career orientation* program. The goal was to provide children with information on the many opportunities available. As an example, in the metalworking industries, there were professional workers, such as engineers of various types with college degrees; technicians, such as tool and die designers, who were probably prepared in two-year technical institutes or community colleges; skilled workers, such as machinists who studied in vocational education and/or apprenticeship programs; semi-skilled persons, such as machine operators, and a diminishing number of unskilled workers with few skills in jobs that often required much physical effort and little thinking.

The orientation program increased youth awareness of work opportunities and provided them with information regarding what was required to become successful in a contemplated career field. Any student interested in becoming a physician would have known that at least seven years of college was required. They would have also known that unique aptitudes were needed to be successful in the health careers field. The orientation period was geared to expanding knowledge of available opportunities in the work world.

Based on Department of Labor codifications, the U. S. Office of Education identified 15 occupational families. These became the foundation for the career orientation program Supported by federal contract monies, materials were prepared that provided pertinent information on the occupations in the 15 families. Also, instructional methodologies, classroom discussion prompts, assigned readings, suggested resource persons from the community, and recommended visits to local businesses, industries, health, and public-service centers were also developed as teacher-friendly resources for the program.

Robert Balthaser, assistant director for Business and Office Education, initially directed the *career exploration* program. The goal of the program was to assist youth to investigate the world of work and cultivate their career interests. This phase of the program was the most difficult to implement. Observation and some hands-on experiences were often the best way for youth to develop or assess their interests. With research on career guidance indicating that career choice did not become reasonable until about age 16, the exploration effort was targeted at the ninth and 10th grades. (Most students turned 16 before the end of their 10th grade year.)

Although the choice of career belonged to the students, the program was designed to encourage them to take a look at the social and economic consequences of their decisions, and to evaluate the talents and educational requirements needed to pursue a chosen career. A manual on goals, procedures, and practices for career exploration was developed in the same manner as for other career development initiatives.

The intent of the career exploration phase was to enable students to make the best use of their last two years in high school. The career education program was not planned as a vocational program. Ohio's vocational education leaders believed simply that students should have a reasonable foundation for making a choice between a vocational program and one leading to preparation in a profession. The program caught the attention of educational leaders statewide. A number of districts initiated planning efforts and the Division of Vocational Education provided funds to local coordinators to assist teachers and principals in implementing the program.

The limited federal funds were insufficient to develop a statewide career education program. Consequently, the state legislature was encouraged to fund expansion of the program. The General Assembly appropriated about $5 million a year for the career education program. With Ohio's commitment to meeting a viable educational need for all young people, the career education program remained a part of the state's public education landscape.

Sidney Marland, director of the U.S. Office of Education, became very interested in the concepts of career education and promoted them nationally. Many states instituted career education efforts using only federal funds, but then saw the federal government move on to other interests.

In 1982, Shoemaker learned that the Ohio Bureau of Employment Services (OBES) was going to stop offering up-to-date information concerning the job market. Believing such information to be very important to both career orientation and career exploration, Shoemaker dispatched Robert Balthaser to meet with OBES to request that the program be transferred to the vocational education division. The transfer was approved. The Ohio Career Information System (OCIS) became the backbone of Ohio's career development program.

Career education began in five school districts in 1969 with career orientation programs in grades seven and eight. The charter districts included Parma, Akron, Toledo, Dayton, and Warren. In 1974, state funded K-10 career education programs included Akron, Benton-Carroll-Salem, Canton, Cincinnati, Clear Fork Valley, Columbus, Dayton, East Muskingum, Geneva, Kirtland, Lorain, Springfield, Mad River Green, Mansfield, Minford, Orville, Parma, South-Western

City in Franklin County, Toledo, Youngstown, Warren, and Willoughby East-lake.

Four regional career education councils were created in 1981 as liaisons to state career education leadership staff to assist in the identification of needs and the coordination of support services.

By 2000, there were career education programs in all 92 Career Technical Planning Districts (CTPDs), serving over 70% of Ohio's K-12 public school population. Every program had a coordinator to assist teachers in organizing and delivering career information. The CTPDs had access to OCIS. OCIS provided career information and other data through compact discs. For $250 a year, CTPDs received the latest information on occupations and other employment related data. The compact discs included occupational information for Ohio and the nation; information on all two-year and four-year colleges in the state and nation (covering everything about the educational institution except course titles); access to the college information regarding location; educational goals; admission requirements; tuition costs; financial aid; job-search information in terms of openings and locations; resume planning; and interview techniques and procedures. The compact discs also contained teacher ideas and information on presenting career information.

Division staff that provided the early leadership to the career education move-ment included Black, K-6; Richard Macer, 7-8; and Robert Balthaser, 9-10. In succession, state career education leadership responsibilities were assigned to Jack Ford, Karen Shylo, Heath, James Cummins, and Cindi Gahris, who currently serves as assistant director for career education.

11

Challenging Years

By 1982, 95% of the statewide framework for vocational education was in place. The Auglaize/Mercer County and Hancock/Paulding County areas were the only places where 11th and 12th grade public school students did not have access to a comprehensive vocational education program. In 1985, creation of the Tri Star and Millstream Vocational Education Compacts completed the statewide plan.

Program access was, however, only part of the vocational education equation in the 1980s. In 1983, the National Commission on Excellence in Education issued its report *A Nation at Risk*. The commission found the nation's public school system inadequate in the areas of math, science, and communications education. *A Nation at Risk* ignited a major debate on school reform. Public education institutions were challenged to do better in preparing students in academic disciplines.

Then, the *1984 Carl D. Perkins Vocational Education Act* emphasized Congress' desire that vocational school graduates have marketable skills. The act sought to improve productivity, and to promote economic growth. It also focused on ensuring that the disadvantaged, persons with disabilities, single parents and homemakers, and those with limited English proficiency had access to vocational training programs. Finally, the law offered assistance to help both men and women enter nontraditional occupations.

PROGRAMS AND SERVICES FOR THE DISADVANTAGED AND PERSONS WITH DISABILITIES

As discussed in Chapter V, Ohio's vocational education system was already addressing some of the concerns raised by the federal legislation and the education reform movement. Vocational special education (VOSE) coordinator services were introduced in the 1978-79 school year. VOSE coordinators, initially funded as classroom units in the joint vocational school districts, worked with vocational teachers and with special education students who were enrolled in vocational education programs. VOSE coordinators provided assistance in formal and informal work evaluation. They helped develop and monitor individualized educational plans (IEPs). They also adapted vocational education curricular materials, training equipment, instructional techniques, and evaluation strategies for special education students who were enrolled in vocational education programs. Another important role of the VOSE coordinator was to serve as the liaison to the home school staff, parents, and other agencies and systems providing services to special education students.

In 1979, the Division of Vocational Education employed Lawrence Dennis to be a liaison with the Special Education Division. Dennis was charged with assisting the integration of special education students into vocational education programs.

In the late 1980s, the Option IV program was introduced in vocational education. Job training coordinators, supported by vocational education dollars, taught this program. They then provided community-based job placement services to low-functioning students with disabilities. These students normally would have been placed in a very limited workshop, or had no employment training options at all.

The success of these various programs was evidenced by the fact that in the 1986-87 school year, 22,662 students with disabilities were enrolled in mainstream vocational education programs. Another 5,954 were enrolled in separate vocational education programs. A total of 15,211 students with disabilities received vocational support services under the *1984 Perkins Act*.

Many disadvantaged students, while not fitting the special education template, were also integrated into vocational education programs. According to the *Fiscal Year 1988 Annual Report of the Ohio Council on Vocational Education*, 52,444 disadvantaged students had enrolled in mainstream vocational education programs the previous year. Another 73,856 disadvantaged students were enrolled in vocational programs designed specifically for that population.

SPECIAL PROGRAMS FOR OTHER TARGETED POPULATIONS

Numerous other job-related educational programs for targeted populations were also spawned in the 1980s. Transitions, a program for dislocated workers, provided job readiness/career transition instruction to 14,047 dislocated workers. Graduation, Reality, and Dual-Role Skills (GRADS), Gaining Opportunities and Living Skills (GOALS), and Displaced Homemaker programs were made available to single parents and homemakers.

The GRADS program was designed for adolescent parents and pregnant adolescents in grades 9-12. The goal was to keep participants in school during pregnancy and after childbirth, and to educate them in infant health care and health-care practices. In the 1986-87 school year, 89 GRADS programs served 3,211 students.

GOALS served single parents (age 17-25) who were high school dropouts and who had sole responsibility for child rearing. The program assisted participants in learning to be effective parents and homemakers. The GOALS program was also designed to encourage participants to complete high school and helped participants find jobs or enroll in vocational training. In 1986-87, seven programs served 347 persons. That same year, 32 programs accommodated the job-related and homemaker education needs of 1,376 displaced homemakers and single heads of households.

Through a set-aside provision in the 1984 federal act, vocational programs and services were also provided to criminal offenders in 11 adult and five youth correctional institutions. In 1986, working in cooperation with the Department of Rehabilitation and Corrections, the Vocational Education Division provided 47 programs to more than 1,500 incarcerated individuals, for both the secondary-level and adult age groups. Follow-up studies found that institutional vocational education for short-term offenders significantly reduced the recidivism rate.

Enacted in 1982, the *Job Training Partnership Act* (JTPA) targeted the preparation of youth and unskilled adults for entry into the labor force, principally by providing cost-free job training to economically disadvantaged individuals, including dislocated workers, and others who faced serious barriers to employment. The U.S. Department of Labor administered JTPA, but the legislation included provisions to utilize in-place education and training facilities for many of the programs and services funded via the act. Subsequently, the Division of

Vocational and Career Education created an Office for Job Training Partnership Services to administer a portion of the education set-aside included in JTPA.

The Jobs for Ohio Graduates (JOG), a program that concentrated on high-risk high school seniors to facilitate their transition from school to work, was one of the initiatives supported with JTPA funds. JOG began in 1986-87. Over the years, the JOG program grew to serve eligible students in grades 9-12, as well as high school dropouts. The in-school program assisted students in making connections between school and work. The dropout program encouraged students to acquire a high school diploma or a GED, as well as gain employment. The Ohio JOG peaked at 14,000 youths and became the largest program of its kind in the country. Funding support for JOG came from various sources, including federal, state, private and foundation dollars.

Twenty percent of the funds included in the JTPA 8% education set-aside were coordinated through the State Education Coordination and Grants Advisory Council (SECGAC). This interagency committee was comprised of representatives from the Board of Regents, JTP Ohio (the governor's advisory body on employment and training), OBES, the Department of Education, and the Department of Health and Human Services. The council identified the types and levels of coordination occurring between local deliverers of JTPA, vocational education, and technical education services and recommend grant allocations to nurture such coordination. Many JTPA eligible clients were mainstreamed into ongoing adult and technical education programs.

THE GOVERNOR'S HUMAN RESOURCE ADVISORY COUNCIL

In 1992, in an attempt to facilitate the coordination of the state's various job-training services, the governor created the Governor's Human Resource Advisory Council (GHRAC). Research on Ohio's job-training initiatives revealed 51 work-development programs directed by 15 different state agencies. GHRAC was to monitor these various training initiatives to minimize duplication of effort and coordinate funding.

Throughout the 1990s, the governor's office worked to bring agencies responsible for workforce development together, and to leverage physical and financial resources for the benefit of all Ohioans. *Forum 2000* listed 17 state agencies with which Career and Technical Education had formal program-coordinating arrangements. Career and technical education had solidified itself as a major player in the state's workforce development system. In 1997, the GHRAC was replaced by the Governor's Workforce Development Board, but program coordination remained a top priority.

EQUITY FOR ALL

The promotion of sex equity was an important provision of the 1976 federal *Vocational Education Amendments.* That goal continued with the passage of the *1984 Perkins Act.* Ohio's vocational education system supported a strong state-wide sex-equity campaign. From the late 1980s on, thousands of pre-vocational, secondary, and adult students benefited from instruction aimed at minimizing sex bias. Still, strong societal forces impeded individuals, especially women, from obtaining employment in what heretofore had been considered a man's world. Such a condition gave rise to a vocational education program known as Orientation to Nontraditional Occupations for Women (ONOW).

With the support of Ohio's business and organized labor communities, this eight-week, pre-employment training program prepared women for jobs in construction, manufacturing, service, and technical occupations. The program provided a valuable resource pool of employable women—women who had a head start in non-traditional occupations. Training was primarily conducted at full-service joint vocational schools, thus making graduates available to employers in virtually every part of the state.

ACADEMIC INTEGRATION

During the 1980s, another significant innovation in vocational education programming included an increased emphasis on and reinforcement of basic academic skills to assure that vocational education students were competent in the areas of math, science, and communications in order to cope with a rapidly changing and increasingly sophisticated workforce.

Pilot projects on the integration of academics into vocational education were conducted in the 1984-85 school year. On July 1, 1985, Program Options was launched. Program Options featured the strategic infusion of academics into job-training program curricula, with appropriately certified academic teachers providing the instruction in their respective disciplines based, in large measure, upon the applied math, science, and communications skills needed by vocational education students in their occupational pursuits, as well as for life-long learning. In many school districts, vocational education students earned math, science, and language arts credits toward graduation as a result of participating in the initiative.

To facilitate the infusion of math and science into vocational education, in 1984 the Division of Vocational and Career Education, in cooperation with 26 other states, joined the Principles of Technology Consortium to participate in and field-test an instructional program model related to teaching the application of 13 physics principles across mechanical, electrical, fluid, and pneumatic systems.

The consortium was precedent setting in two ways. First, it was the first national vocational education collaboration among states to pool resources to develop an instructional model. Second, while the model was developed in close collaboration with the vocational education community, it was designed and written by renowned scientists who had a keen awareness of and commitment to a new approach to teaching science in the context of the world of work.

This collaborative effort was so successful that similar national consortium initiatives followed. They included one in applied math and another in applied biology and chemistry. Vocational education was rapidly being viewed as not only an end (that is preparing people for work), but a means to the end (offering an instructional approach that facilitated the teaching and application of key academic principles). To that end, on July 11, 1988, the State Board of Education approved a new standard that provided funding for academic classes in joint vocational schools.

SCANS

While academic infusion into vocational education was becoming somewhat commonplace by the late 1980s, another phenomenon was becoming obvious to workforce educators. In 1991, the U.S. Department of Labor released a report entitled, *The Secretary's Commission on Achieving Necessary Skills* (SCANS). It challenged schools to teach five categories of competencies that were pervasive throughout the workforce. Those competencies were to be woven through a complex interplay in the teaching of basic skills, higher order skills, and the application of selected personal qualities. The five competencies, also known as workforce know-how, included the abilities to:

1. identify, organize, plan, and allocate resources such as time, money, materials and facilities,

2. work with others,

3. acquire and use information,

4. understand complex interrelationships, and

5. work with a variety of technologies.

These competencies seemed to have a natural fit with vocational education as acknowledged by Dr. Franklin B. Walter, state superintendent of Public Instruction. During an ODE cabinet meeting, Walter said, *Vocational education is the only program in our public education system that is addressing these competencies. Vocational education is not only teaching these competencies in the classroom and laboratory, but they epitomize what the vocational student organizations are all about.* Once again, vocational education seemed to be on target in addressing the educational needs of successful workers beyond the provision of just occupational skills.

TECH PREP

Following on the heels of the applied academics movement in vocational education in Ohio, new federal vocational education legislation was enacted. This legislation, which amended the *Carl D. Perkins Vocational Education Act of 1984*, was entitled the *Carl D. Perkins Vocational and Applied Technology Act Amendments of 1990.*

One of the act's provisions was Tech Prep, a competency based education and career-oriented program. It included a common core of required proficiencies in mathematics, science, communications, and technologies that would lead to an associate degree, or a two-year certificate in a specific career field. To put it another way, Tech Prep was a federally funded articulation agreement that allowed high school students to earn credits acceptable toward career-focused, two-year associate degrees at a state college.

This 2+2 educational concept proposed a seamless curriculum beginning in the 11th grade. It culminated with an associate degree at the end of two years of career-focused education at one of the state's two-year state colleges.

A portion of the basic grants to states could be used to launch the Tech Prep initiative; however, the law lacked any definition of Tech Prep or conditions that had to be met in justifying the expenditure of the funds.

From the beginning of the Tech Prep movement in Ohio, representatives from the Board of Regents and the Department of Education agreed that this would not be "just another federal program," one that mysteriously disappeared after federal dollars were no longer available. Concentrated efforts were made to design a Tech Prep program fulfilling the law's intent and meeting the needs of a unique population in the last two years of Ohio's public high schools, namely, those who were career-focused and demonstrated the academic and technical aptitudes to be successful in such a program.

State college officials, local vocational education administrators, business leaders, and representatives from organized labor were engaged in dialogues to more precisely define Tech Prep and the characteristics of a Tech Prep program template. A vision of Tech Prep evolved that addressed six components:

1. Tech Prep would promote systemic changes in curricular content, admissions policies and course credit acquisition at both the high school and community college levels.

2. Tech Prep would provide for expanded student opportunities to explore and participate in career focused educational programs.

3. Tech Prep would provide for early individual career education opportunities to assist students and parents in making informed career choices.

4. Tech Prep would be based on formal partnerships between secondary education, postsecondary education, business, industry, and organized labor.

5. The Tech Prep curriculum would include the teaching of academic, occupational, and employability content. Students would possess demonstrable occupational competencies at any point of exit.

6. Tech Prep students would demonstrate advanced academic and technical knowledge and skills defined by business and industry at the end of a two-year associate degree, school-to-work, or apprenticeship program.

As of 1997, 28 Tech Prep consortia—each consisting of at least one VEPD, one two-year postsecondary institution, and business, industry, and organized labor partners—had been organized in Ohio. Forty-three colleges, universities, and regional campuses; 91 vocational planning districts; more than 400 secondary school districts, and more than 600 business, industry and labor representatives were actively involved in the consortia.

ANSWERING THE CHALLENGE

The many and varied initiatives on the state's vocational education agenda in the 80's did not go for naught, as evidenced by the following FY 92 facts. At the secondary level:

- More than half (55%) of Ohio's 11th and 12th graders—128,249 students were enrolled in secondary vocational education.

- Thirty percent of Ohio's 11th and 12th graders, or 71,464 students were enrolled in secondary job training programs.

- Vocational education programs served 68,608 disadvantaged students and 23,491 disabled students.

- Vocational education served 1,842 secondary students in Ohio correctional institutions.

- Funds from the 8% JTPA served 4,422 young adults.

- The unemployment figure for people age 21 and younger was 7.7% for completers of secondary vocational job training programs as compared to 18.1% in the civilian labor force generally.

At the postsecondary level:

- Students enrolled in adult vocational education totaled 68,833 in full-time programs and 164,298 in part-time programs.

- Unemployed workers who enrolled in adult vocational education programs were re-employed after training at a 96% rate.

- Skill training was available to 100% of Ohio's adult population.

- Targeted populations such as dislocated workers, displaced homemakers, and the economically disadvantaged accounted for 46% (31,642) of the enrollment in full-time adult programs.

- Vocational education served 1,917 adults in Ohio's correctional institutions.

- The U.S. Department of Education designated Ohio's 32 adult vocational education full-service centers as skill clinics that were called for in the national education publication *America 2000*. The full-service centers offered training and support services for 103,398 individuals and 1,441 businesses.

Vocational education had clearly met the challenge.

12

Age of Accountability

In 1984, the State Board of Education adopted *Indicators of Progress* designed to strengthen elementary and secondary education, and encourage local educational systems to report annually on their status in relation to such indicators.

Reflecting on that, former state board President Richard Glowacki stated:

> *The* Indicators of Progress *was a first move toward accountability by a major state department and, in its time, was greatly applauded. It was one of the incremental steps to get to the kind of accountability that we are thinking about today.*

Twelve major areas of educational concern were addressed in *Indicators of Progress.* One in particular addressed vocational education. It related to the percentage of high school graduates completing vocational education programs, and to the percentage of vocational education graduates placed in jobs and in occupations for which they were trained.

Accountability, however, was nothing new to vocational education in Ohio or elsewhere across the nation. Federal legislation had required annual reporting of placement rates and other accountability outcomes for many years. For example, the federal government was continuously collecting information regarding the effect that vocational education had on youth unemployment.

In reference to that concern, in fiscal year 1991, the overall unemployment figure for people age 21 and younger in the civilian labor force was 18.1%. That same year, the unemployment rate for secondary vocational education program completers in Ohio was 7.7%, less than half the rate for Ohio's general population cohort (Ohio Comprehensive Annual Report, fiscal year 1992). In addition, the annual adult unemployment rate for vocational education participants was much lower than the general unemployment rate for the state.

CORE STANDARDS AND PERFORMANCE MEASURES

With the advent of the *Carl D. Perkins Vocational and Applied Technology Act of 1990*, additional accountability responsibilities were placed upon vocational education. Section 2 of the act stated:

> ... *[I]t is the purpose of this Act to make the United States more competitive in the world economy by developing more fully the academic and occupational skills of all segments of the population. This purpose will principally be achieved through concentrating resources on improving educational programs leading to academic and occupational skill competencies needed to work in a technologically advanced society.*

The law made it clear that the intent of Congress was to insure that "all segments" of the population should have access to occupational education programs that prepared individuals for careers in demand, currently as well as in the future.

In compliance with the Perkins' legislation, the Division of Vocational and Adult Education provided the leadership and coordination in developing a set of core standards and performance measures that would create access and success opportunities for the populations targeted by the act. The process for developing such standards and measures was comprehensive, both in the scope of the standards and measures, and among the stakeholders that played roles in their development.

Core standards specified the criteria in terms of what was to be measured, and set the targeted levels of achievement for the respective standards. Performance measures set forth when and how each standard was to be measured. The VEPDs were then responsible for reporting each year to the division the outcomes for each standard. The VEPDs were also to use the information and data from outcomes to develop their annual plans. The standards and measures built upon the already successful practices established by each institution.

The initial core standards and performance measures for Ohio included the following components:

- Parent and student access to career information and employment opportunities through vocational education,
- Academic learning and competency gains,

- Occupational learning and competency gains,

- Work and family life learning and competency gains,

- Placement,

- Enrollment and retention, and

- Career development

The establishment of core standards and performance measures in vocational education required revamping the state-designed program evaluation approach from one that focused primarily on process to one more oriented toward how students performed relative to levels of achievement in their respective program areas. To that end, a new evaluation strategy, Measuring and Planning Progress (MaPP), was designed. It focused on student outcomes.

The MaPP evaluation initiative used a Strategic Analysis Team made up of representatives from local businesses, industries, and agencies to evaluate programs and make recommendations for program improvement, disinvestment, and expansion. During fiscal year 1992, secondary level MaPP evaluations involved 21 VEPDs and 87 participating schools. A total of 370 committees comprised of 3,075 members, who analyzed programs based upon student achievement, progress, and need took part.

STATEWIDE COMPETENCY TESTING

In addition to core standards and performance measures, the *1990 Perkins Act* required states to develop measures of learning and competency gains. These measures would assist in the continuous improvement of vocational education.

Coincidentally, Ohio's 10-year strategic *Plan to Accelerate the Modernization of Vocational Education (Ohio's Future at Work)* also called for increased accountability by vocational programs and students. Ohio's initiative fit hand in glove with the federal mandate for improved accountability in vocational education.

Given that the primary purpose of vocational education was the preparation of students for future employment, measures of assessing occupational competence became the basis for the accountability system. The assessment initiative built on occupational competency analysis profiles (OCAPs), a process that had already identified lists of occupation-specific academic, occupational, and employability skills. The assessment was designed to measure the levels of learning of those essential skills in the respective program areas.

Enlisting the services of representatives from business and industry along with that of vocational teachers, test-writing panels developed 39 different occupational tests. Each test item was scrutinized by professional test writers and subjected to a psychometric evaluation to assure validity and reliability. The first tests were made available statewide in 1994.

The OCAP Assessment package had two components, an occupational and an employability skills assessment. Academic competency assessment was accomplished through the use of *Work Keys,* a work-based academic assessment scheme designed by American College Testing. *Work Keys* tests were part of Ohio's competency assessment plan. They measured individual student academic competencies in three different areas—locating information, applied math, and applied technology, or reading for information, depending upon which occupational area was being tested.

For example, vocational students in the craft areas were tested in applied technology. Vocational students studying business and marketing were assessed in reading for information. The cost per student of administering and scoring each OCAP Assessment test was $6.50. Administering the *Work Keys* component added $10.05 to the cost.

This tandem approach to assessment was the first of its kind in the nation. The test and measurement professionals at the Ohio Vocational Instructional Materials Laboratory at The Ohio State University designed the OCAP Assessment package. It was copied by at least one other state. Perhaps as important, the center's professionals became widely known for their expertise in developing competency assessment instruments. They were often called upon to design testing strategies and materials for in-state and out-of-state governmental agencies and licensing boards.

Since the introduction of the OCAP Assessment and *Work Keys* competency test package in 1994, the federal government has mandated the use of high stakes academic assessment as the performance measure. In light of that mandate, Ohio began using state proficiency test data in lieu of *Work Keys* to measure the academic performance of secondary vocational students. *Work Keys*, however, continued to be used at the postsecondary level. Academic, occupational, and employability competency test results were, and still are, incorporated into each vocational student's career passport.

SKILL STANDARDS

In 1994, the National Skills Standards Board (NSSB) was created to build a voluntary national system of skill standards assessment and certification systems to enhance the ability of the United States workforce to compete effectively in a global economy. These skills were to be identified by industry in full partnership with labor, civil rights groups, and community-based organizations. These standards were to be based on high-performance work and were to be portable across 15 industry sectors.

The board's mission was:

- To promote the growth of high-performance work organizations in the private and public sectors that operate on the basis of productivity, quality, and innovation, and—in the private sector—profitability;

- To raise the standard of living and economic security of American workers by improving access to high-skill, high-wage employment and career opportunities for those in, entering, or re-entering the workforce; and

- To encourage the use of world-class academic, occupational, and employability standards to guide education and training for current and future workers.

However, Ohio's Career and Technical Education enterprise was heavily immersed in skill standards long before the arrival of the NSSB. Although not national in scope, the 64 Ohio Competency Analysis Profiles (discussed in more detail in Chapter XIII, The Modernization Era) were high-performance skill standards identified by Ohio's workforce.

Moreover, since 1983, career and technical education in Ohio had been working closely with the automotive repair industry to incorporate that industry's standards into its programs in automotive technology, collision repair and refinish, and medium/heavy truck repair training. In fact, Ohio had one of the first three training programs in the nation (the Tri-county JVS automotive mechanics program at Nelsonville) to be recognized by the Institute for Automotive Service Excellence (ASE) for meeting industry standards for training automobile repair technicians.

Nationally, automotive repair training program certification was, and still is, voluntary. But, in 1989, Ohio mandated that automotive repair training programs administered by the state Career/Technical and Adult Education (CTAE) Office were to become ASE certified. Programs had a five-year window to become certified. After that time, only certified programs would continue to receive state-allocated funding subsidies.

To say the least, local school administrators and automotive technology teachers did not enthusiastically endorse such a mandate. But the process moved forward, and within the five-year time frame, all secondary and postsecondary automotive training programs had achieved ASE certification. At the time of this writing, the number of certified automotive repair programs in Ohio included 102 in automobile service and repair, 49 in collision repair and refinish, and nine in medium/heavy truck repair. Ohio had nearly 11% of all such certified programs in the country, more than any other state.

Today, automotive repair teachers across the state will testify that even though they did not readily accept the program certification mandate, *it was probably the best thing that could have happened.* The mandate focused the curriculum and investment of resources (time and money). The result was significant program improvement and a higher caliber technician entering the workforce.

THE GHAZALAH STUDY

Unlike any other educational endeavor, the economic performance of vocational education graduates was, and still is, a primary factor in the evaluation of vocational education programs. In part to address this concern, in 1986 the Division of Vocational and Adult Education contracted with Dr. L. A. Ghazalah, professor of economics at Ohio University, to conduct a longitudinal study of vocational education graduates from the class of 1979. The study evaluated the wage-earning performance of students who completed state-funded vocational job training programs in Ohio.

Using original source information and data (federal income tax records provided by the Internal Revenue Service), the study examined the performance over time of 15,055 1979 graduates of 14 vocational programs. Twelve of the programs, with 13,109 graduates, were at the secondary level. Two programs, with 1,946 graduates, were at the associate degree (second year college) level. This study compared the incomes of 1979 graduates in 1983, 1984, 1985, and 1986, to those in the general population of the same age, educational attainment level, and geographic location. The study was the first of its kind in the nation.

The results indicated predominantly higher incomes for vocational graduates compared to others in the general population of the same age and with comparable years of schooling. Results varied by vocational program, but vocational graduates showed significant wage-earning advantages each year over the four years studied. Furthermore, the 1979 graduates showed a general widening of the margin in 1986 compared to 1985, 1984, and 1983 between their incomes and the incomes of the comparable group in the general population.

The Ghazalah Study, as it became known, received national acclaim. It was recognized in *USA Today* as well as in numerous federal releases and documents. Even other states referenced the study to document the economic effect of vocational education wage earners.

13

Modernization Era

In 1989, the 118th General Assembly passed *Amended Substitute Senate Bill 140*. Section 3313.901 stated that *the State Board shall prepare a plan of action for accelerating the modernization of the vocational curriculum ... that can furnish students with the ... skills needed to participate successfully in the work force of the future*. The act authorized the state board to reform curriculum, allocate personnel and resources, and develop new standards and strategies.

SB140 came about as a result of fundamental issues in Ohio's economy. Would Ohio's future workforce have what it takes to compete in a world economy? Who would handle business and industry's needs for an educated and productive work force? How could vocational and career education become more accessible to increased numbers of secondary and adult students?

Answering these and other questions fell on the shoulders of Ohio's vocational education system. Vocational education leaders were being challenged to develop new and innovative solutions; to turn obstacles into opportunities; and to be more vigorous in improving the design and delivery of vocational and career education programs and services of value to all youth and adult students.

In response, Ohio's vocational education leaders set in motion a process that culminated in the publication of *Ohio's Future at Work,* a commitment to do what was necessary to shape vocational and career education for the next decade.

Dr. Robert E. Taylor, former executive director of the National Center for Research in Vocational Education and professor emeritus at The Ohio State University, led the planning. A 40-member, statewide Modernization Forum convened in Columbus on three occasions to deliberate and shape the plan. The forum consisted of representatives from the Ohio Chamber of Commerce, the Ohio Manufacturers' Association, the Ohio Farm Bureau, the Bureau of Apprenticeship Training, organized labor, the business community, public and higher education, and the news media.

The forum considered a broad array of environmental forces and trends influ-encing vocational education, including economic and employment conditions, demographic factors, and educational reform initiatives. It became clear that expectations for vocational and career education had been heightened. New alli-ances would have to be forged among education, vocational education, business, industry, labor, and community and governmental agencies to respond to envi-ronmental forces and trends, and to assure the full benefits of modern life for all citizens.

Six regional meetings were held around the state to share the forum's progress and to get input. Nineteen discussion papers were submitted by various groups interested in vocational education's future.

Drafting a revised mission statement was central to redefining vocational edu-cation. The statement drafted by the forum stated:

> The mission of the vocational and career education system is to prepare youths and adults in an efficient and timely fashion, to make informed choices and to success-fully enter, compete, and advance in a changing world of work. This broadened mission will be achieved in concert with educational and business communities by offering comprehensive education, training, and support services that develop the following:
>
> - Occupational skills—those skills involving the technical abilities to per-form required workplace tasks, including problem solving and critical thinking.
>
> - Academic skills—those core competencies necessary to prepare for and secure a career, facilitate lifelong learning, and assure success in a global economy.
>
> - Employability skills—those personal development and leadership abilities essential for increased productivity, economic self-sufficiency, career flexi-bility, business ownership, and effective management of work and family commitments.

The modernization plan was structured around 11 imperatives that served as the foundation for ongoing educational reform and revitalization, and provided benchmarks for measuring progress.

The imperatives were:

1. Broaden the scope of the vocational education experience for each student.

2. Improve access to enhanced educational opportunities.

3. *Emphasize rigorous outcomes for vocational students and programs.*

4. *Focus on the life-long learning needs of individuals.*

5. *Provide career-focused education for all students.*

6. *Modify and streamline vocational education standards, guidelines and policies.*

7. *Assure adequate resources and their efficient utilization.*

8. *Accelerate professional development of vocational educators.*

9. *Extend and strengthen vocational education's strategic alliances.*

10. *Enhance the public's understanding of, and support for, vocational education.*

11. *Maintain constant emphasis on improving and renewing the vocational education system.*

Over a six-month period, *Ohio's Future at Work* took shape and was presented to the State Board of Education for consideration on June 11, 1990. Coupled with the *1990 Perkins Act*, the goals of *Ohio's Future at Work* had a profound effect on the state's vocational and career education system.

INDIVIDUAL CAREER PLAN (ICP)

Each student will have an individual career plan that is based on an assessment of interests, aptitudes, abilities, and achievement and will be used to advise the students regarding career paths and course selection. (Imperative Four, Objective One in *Ohio's Future at Work*).

The State Board of Education endorsed the concept of an ICP for <u>all</u> students, to be initiated at the eighth grade, to be updated annually through graduation. To that end, the board recommended appropriations in the state biennium budget for subsidies to local school districts to encourage them to implement the ICP program. By 1995, 92% of 131,787 eighth graders had ICPs, and 91.4% of 117,539 ninth graders had reviewed and updated their ICPs.

The ICP became a popular career guidance tool for both vocational and college prep students. It received national acclaim and other states adopted it in its entirety or adapted it to their specific needs.

OCCUPATIONAL COMPETENCY ANALYSIS PROFILES (OCAP)

In Imperative 3, one objective was to develop a comprehensive and employer-verified competency list for each vocational program. Sixty-four employer/incumbent worker-verification committees—involving almost 800 business owners, craftsmen, and educators—reviewed specific occupational, academic and employability competencies and identified new ones that would be needed by the emerging workforce. All the competencies were then incorporated into OCAP booklets. Local program advisory committees used the booklets to verify courses of study or to modify them to address specific needs of community-based business and industry. OCAPs found their way into 46 other states and six foreign countries.

OHIO COMPETENCY ASSESSMENT PROGRAM

A natural follow-up to the OCAP initiative was an objective associated with Imperative 4. The objective stated:

> *Each completer of a vocational program will have an individual career passport that enables him or her to pursue work and/or lifelong learning and that includes items such as documented work and/or community experiences; a student profile establishing performance or competency levels; leadership experiences; attendance records; an outline of continuing education needs; and career credentialing.*

The Ohio Competency Assessment Program, a paper and pencil testing program, addressed the student competency profile. It measured student knowledge and understanding of the employer/employee-verified competencies identified through the OCAP process.

CAREER PASSPORT

The *Career Passport* was also an outgrowth of *Ohio's Future at Work*. The passport was a portfolio containing formal documents describing the marketable skills of the vocational completer as defined by the Division of Vocational and Career Education. It was designed to assist students in making the transition from school to work, job seeking, and career planning by documenting skills and knowledge acquired through work and non-work experiences.

> *The Career Passport addresses the need to identify and document the employability, occupational, and academic skills of vocational completers. For students, it is a tool to be utilized in any situation that calls for a resume or concise description of an individual's skills and abilities (e.g., when interviewing, job searching, or completing applications). For employers, colleges, and training institutions, it provides information for screening, interviewing, and selecting applicants.*

Some 500 high school students and adults piloted the passport in 1991-92. Vocational education programs statewide began using it in the next school year. The concept was so enthusiastically endorsed that then State Superintendent Ted Sanders encouraged its use in all public high schools. At its peak, more than 100,000 career passports were being used in Ohio's high schools. Other states requested permission to either use Ohio's career passport model, or adapt it to their needs.

THE OHIO VOCATIONAL EDUCATION LEADERSHIP INSTITUTE

Another important outgrowth of *Ohio's Future at Work* was the creation of the Ohio Vocational Education Leadership Institute (OVELI). Imperative 11 emphasized improving and renewing the vocational education system. OVELI's mission was to assure a reliable flow of proven candidates for leadership positions in vocational education at the local and state level.

Specifically, the institute aimed to:

1. *Assure an adequate number of high-quality leaders. These are vocational educators who, through their studies, job experiences, selection and completion of the institute program, will have completed the performance requirements for new or replacement state and local leadership positions.*

2. *Assure continuity of administrative leadership and improve program performance and stability through effective leadership at the state and local level.*

3. *Assure high-level administrator performance, cost efficiency and compliance with relevant standards and regulations in program operations.*

4. *Contribute <u>intellectual capital</u> to the state vocational education programs through projects of the institute's fellows and seminar sessions.*

5. *Prepare vocational education <u>statesmen</u>. These are educators who are both competent and comfortable in a variety of settings and jurisdictions, including local and state leadership roles and working with legislators, professional associations, and other constituencies.*

6. *Provide the state division of vocational education with a <u>quick response network</u> to rapidly mobilize talent, provide useful inputs and marshal political support on key issues.*

7. *Provide a <u>policy advisory network</u> to the Division of Vocational Education by serving as a "sounding board" for policy options and program initiatives in the formative stages.*

Under the direction of Charlotte Coomer in the Division of Vocational and Adult Education, the year-long program was designed, in large measure, to develop individuals competent to lead and manage programs, as well as to provide leadership in program innovation and to be influential in local, state, and national decisions that shaped vocational and career education in Ohio.

Originally intended to have a five-year life, OVELI (later changed to the Ohio Career Technical Education Leadership Institute (OCTELI)) had, as of 2000, 10 classes of more than 240 fellows completing the year-long program.

14

Ohio's Future at Work: Beyond 2000

On January 1, 1995, Dr. Darrell Parks, who had directed Ohio's vocational education program since 1982, retired. In August, Dr. Joanna Kister became division director. She began planning for vocational and adult education in the 21st century.

Building on *Ohio's Future at Work*, Ohio's *Future at Work: Beyond 2000* provided a new direction that expanded the mission for vocational and adult education. It included changing the name to career and technical education(CTE). The goal was to meet *the life-long learning needs of Ohio's youth and adults as well as the ever-changing demands of the present and future workforce.*

Ohio's Future at Work: Beyond 2000 identified four priorities. The first was to expand options for achieving career and technical education goals via career pathways through a sequence of academic, technological, occupational coursework, and other educational experiences leading to a career specialty. *Career Pathways* complemented the Tech Prep model that was discussed in Chapter XI. It provided a seamless program of studies beginning in high school and leading to an associate's degree with advanced mathematics, science, communications, and technical competencies.

Career Pathways was the umbrella initiative. From the pioneering efforts of career education specialists to implementation of the concept at sites across the state, *Career Pathways* expanded the concept of career education. It guided thousands of students and parents toward more informed career choices, and improved the preparation of students for employment in a high-tech/high-performance workforce.

Taking its lead from national movements that were targeting the preparation of tomorrow's workforce, the overall curriculum framework for CTE was modified to better match the economic and employment patterns of Ohio's workforce. The CTE curricular model was built around 16 career fields.

- <u>Agricultural and Environmental Science</u>—Includes technical and professional-level careers in animal and crop production; agricultural services and engineering; food processing; horticulture; natural resources management; environmental services, and agricultural environmental education, communications and research.

- <u>Arts and Communications</u>—Includes technical and professional-level careers related to the humanities and the performing, visual, literary, and media arts.

- <u>Business and Administrative Services</u>—Includes technical and professional-level careers in business management, administrative support, human resources, and business administration that encompass planning, organizing, directing, and evaluating business functions essential to efficient and productive business operations. Business management and administrative services career opportunities are available in every sector of the economy.

- <u>Construction Technologies</u>—Includes technical and professional-level careers in designing, planning, managing, and building and maintaining the built environment, including roadways and bridges and industrial, commercial, and residential facilities and buildings.

- <u>Education and Training</u>—Includes technical and professional-level careers in planning, managing, and providing education and training services and related learning support services.

- <u>Engineering and Science Technologies</u>—Includes technical and professional-level careers in: (a) planning, managing, and providing scientific research and services such as laboratory and testing and research and development; (b) design, process, and development services such as electrical engineering, industrial engineering, materials science, nanofabrication, fuel cell technology, and robotics.

- <u>Finance</u>—Includes technical and professional-level careers in financial and investment planning, accounting, banking, insurance, real estate, and business financial management.

- <u>Government and Public Administration</u>—Includes technical and professional-level careers in national defense, foreign service, governance, revenue and taxation, regulation, and public administration at local, state and federal levels.

- <u>Health Science</u>—Includes technical and professional-level careers in planning, managing, and providing therapeutic services, diagnostic services, health informatics, support services, and biotechnology research and development.

- <u>Hospitality and Tourism</u>—Includes technical and professional-level careers in the management, marketing, and operations of restaurants and other food services, lodging, attractions, recreation events and travel-related services.

- <u>Human Services</u>—Includes technical and professional-level careers related to families and human needs within economic, political, and social services, counseling and mental health services, consumer services and personal-care services.

- <u>Information Technology</u>—Includes technical and professional-level careers in the design, development, and support and management of hardware, software, multimedia and systems integration services. (Occupations where workers use computer systems or software, but do not design, develop, implement or support the system are not included in this career field.)

- <u>Law & Public Safety</u>—Includes technical and professional-level careers in planning, managing, and providing judicial, legal, public administration, public safety and protective services, and homeland security including professional and technical support services in public planning, emergency management planning, fire protection, emergency medical services, and the criminal justice system.

- <u>Manufacturing Technologies</u>—Includes technical and professional-level careers in planning, managing, and performing the processing of materials into intermediate or final products and related professional and technical support activities such as production planning and control, maintenance, and manufacturing/process engineering.

- <u>Marketing</u>—Includes technical and professional-level careers in planning, managing, and performing marketing activities such as distribution, promotion, pricing, selling, financing, information management, and product/service management to reach organizational objectives.

- <u>Transportation Systems</u>—Includes technical and professional-level careers in planning, management, and movement of people, materials and goods by road, pipeline, air, rail, and water, and related professional and technical support services such as transportation infrastructure planning and management, logistics services and mobile equipment and facility maintenance services.

Since its inception in 1991, as discussed in Chapter XI, Tech Prep in Ohio continued to grow in scope and importance. It was predicted that in the changing job market, 75% of all occupations would require some postsecondary education. Most of those jobs would also require technical skills.

In the 1998-99 school year, 7,575 Tech Prep students were enrolled in Ohio's secondary and two-year college tech prep programs. Governor Bob Taft set a goal of 35,000 Tech Prep students by 2003.

The second priority of *Ohio's Future at Work: Beyond 2000* was to *strengthen teaching and learning.* That was to be accomplished through:

- *Professional development designed to provide teachers ongoing professional growth opportunities, including workshops, field trips, conferences, seminars and a leadership institute.*

- *Statewide participation in High Schools That Work (HSTW), a national high school reform model designed to link high-quality academic and high-quality technical studies.*

- *The integration of technical and academic competencies (ITAC), combining academic, technical and employability skills into core, cluster and specialty competencies.*

The Ohio Career-Technical Education Leadership Institute (OCTELI), formerly OVELI, continued in the 1990s to offer exemplary leadership development experiences and opportunities to CTE professionals. Including the class of 2000 fellows, the institute graduated more than 240 educators in a decade.

HSTW became an integrating force for *Ohio's Future at Work: Beyond 2000.* It emphasized linking high-quality academic and high-quality technical studies. Ten key practices provided models and resources to eliminate the general track and strengthen the quality of instruction.

Also, Ohio's CTE program complemented the Ohio Department of Education's commitment to raising academic and technical standards. CTE aligned its curricula with the state academic standards. The ITAC framework focused on contextual teaching and learning and ITAC resource guides were developed for instructional program leaders and teachers. One of the resource guides, *Ohio's itWORKS*, was an information technology program that became a model for the national career cluster project.

Ohio's Future at Work: Beyond 2000's third priority, to *enhance communications and collaboration* was to be achieved through:

- *Website communication, including up-to-date fact sheets, background information, and a monthly newsletter;*

- *Video, audio, and print communications to be shared with educators and policy makers, and*

- *Collaboration between academic and technical educators; the secondary and postsecondary systems, and among educators; the business community; and the statewide workforce development system.*

Priority three aimed to build links among professional associations, business leaders, policy boards, state legislators, and members of Congress. Regular electronic communications with the field became standard fare for the CTAE state office.

Collaborative efforts included partnerships with the construction technology industry, the community college system, and a solid working relationship with the Governor's Workforce Policy Board.

Priority four focused on the *promotion of continuous improvement and innovation*. Tools for addressing this priority included:

- *Performance measures such as attendance, placement, and technical competency.*

- *High academic achievement for career-technical education students as measured by state proficiency tests.*

- *High levels of occupational preparedness as measured by statewide occupational performance assessment instruments.*

- *The use of Malcolm Baldrige Quality Award of ISO 9000 criteria.*

Utilizing the Baldrige framework for high performance, the new Ohio profile "performance snapshot" documented five years of improvement in career and technical education programs. Data on performance measures included post-program placement (95.3%), related employment (73.6%), and continuing education (40.3%). HSTW data also presented major challenges in improving career-tech students' reading skills. The commitment to continuous improvement was a valuable tool for program planning and resource allocation.

APPENDIX A

Standards for Vocational Education

The following standards for vocational education plans and programs in Ohio were adopted by the State Board of Education at its January 1970 meeting.

Standard EDb-463-01

Each plan must provide for vocational education for eligible students based upon the following percentages by September 1, 1974:

Percent of graduates entering college or degree-granting higher education programs	Percentage of students for whom vocational education will be planned by September 1, 1974
50% or less	40%
50-60%	30%
60-70%	20%
70% or more	10%

Standard EDb-463-02

The proposed plan shall provide for a minimum of 12 different vocational education offerings providing 20 classes under the Foundation program, with no more than four of these offerings to be provided by cooperative education methods.

Standard EDB-463-03

All plans shall include provisions for vocational education services to all districts or combination of districts within individual county or multi-county areas represented in the plan. All programs proposed to meet the minimum standards for vocational education shall meet the criteria for vocational education programs as approved by the State Board of Education.

Standard EDb-463-04

No school district or combination of school districts shall be considered for the allocation of construction, remodeling and equipment funds from state or federal sources unless such a district or combination of districts has a minimum of 1,500 students in the upper four years of school. Because of the limitation of funds, districts or combination of districts with a minimum of 3,000 students in the upper four years will be given priority.

Standard EDb-463-05

Any plan submitted on the basis of contracting districts shall include:

A.   The provision for physical facilities for the vocational programs by one or more of the boards of education with one participating school providing for no less than 10 programs and 16 classes.

B.   The tax source for building needed vocational facilities and an agreement that each district will guarantee to pay a participation fee for students annually to the district which will be offering the vocational education program based upon the following formula:

1.   Districts enrolling 60% or less of its graduates in degree granting higher education programs will guarantee to pay a participation fee to the district or districts which will be offering the vocational education program for a minimum of 20% of the 11th and 12th grade enrollment.

2.   Districts enrolling 61 to 75% of its graduates in degree-granting higher education programs will guarantee to pay a participation fee to the district or districts offering the vocational education program for a minimum of 15% of the 11th and 12th grade enrollment.

3.   Districts enrolling 76 to 90% of its graduates in degree-granting higher education programs will guarantee to pay a participation fee to the district or districts offering the vocational education program for a minimum of 10% of the 11th and 12th grade enrollment.

4.   Districts enrolling 91% or more of its graduates in degree-granting higher education programs will guarantee to pay a participation fee to the district or districts offering the vocational education program for a minimum of 5% of the 11th and 12th grade enrollment.

5. Districts that develop a cooperative plan for providing vocational education programs, in which provisions other than (1) through (4) above are desirable, may establish mutually agreeable fiscal arrangements. Fiscal arrangements shall be stated in the plan.

6. The initial contract arrangements between boards of education under this section shall be for no less than five years, renewable on the basis of five-year periods. Contracts between boards of education, however, in cases where one board of education has obligated funds for the construction and for equipping of vocational education facilities, must cover a period of years necessary to amortize the obligation.

    Any change in contractual arrangements during the life of the contract must have the approval of the participating districts and the State Board of Education.

    Participating districts are responsible to pay participation fees based upon the formula above, even though less than the formula number of students participate in vocational classes in the vocational center.

Standard EDb-463-06

The county superintendent, the joint vocational school superintendent where the jointure exists, and the superintendent of the city enrolling the largest number of students within the county shall be charged with establishing a committee including representation from all school districts in the county or counties to develop a plan for the county or in cooperation with one or more of the adjoining counties. The county superintendent shall be responsible for arranging the first meeting with the superintendents from the city and the joint vocational school districts in or to initiate the planning. The county superintendent of the most populous county in each vocational district identified in the broad plan proposed by the Governor's Committee on Vocational Education shall take the initiative in contacting the county superintendents of the other counties to arrange a meeting of the districts encompassed in the area. At the first general meeting of superintendents arranged by the committee outlined above, a chairman shall be elected by the group. The elected chairman shall be responsible for coordinating the districts involved. The planning committee for vocational education may establish such additional committees and planning activities as are deemed advisable.

Standard EDb-463-07

The legal base for planning procedure, standards, and other materials shall be transmitted to all superintendents in Ohio before the 20th of the month in which standards are adopted by the State Board.

Standard EDb-463-08

Planning committees are to be initiated by all districts or combination of districts, counties or multi-county units not later than the 15th of the month following receipt of the planning materials.

Standard EDb-463-09

Plans must be submitted to the State Board of Education in accordance with the provisions of Section 3313.90 R.C. by April 1, 1970.

Standard EDb-463-10

Plans shall be reviewed by the Division of Vocational Education in terms of the standards for districting. Adjustments shall be made in the plans in cooperation with the local education agencies and recommendations made to the State Board concerning the plans no later than June 8, 1970.

Standard EDb-463-11

Plans from an individual district or combination of districts, a single county or multi-counties may be submitted to the State Board of Education any time after the approval of the planning procedures, providing such procedures are submitted to the State Department of Education, Division of Vocational Education, by the 15th of the month prior to the month in which they are to be considered by the State Board of Education. The State Board, upon the recommendation of the Superintendent of Public Instruction, and upon determining that the plans meet the standards for districting, may approve the plan submitted, and make the districts eligible for operations allocations, construction and equipment allocations, or both.

Standard EDb-463-12

State Board procedures for the approval of requests for construction and equipment funds and for the submission of these requests for approval of the State Board of Control shall be as follows:

A. Funds shall not be allocated until the district or area plan for Vocational Education has been approved by the State Board of Education.

B. After approval of a request for funds by the State Board of Education, a request shall be made for the State Board of Control for release of funds for the project.

C. Any district adversely affected by the determination of the Division of Vocational Education or action of the State Board of Education may follow the procedure for appeal as outlined in Chapter 119 R.C.

D. Procedures for applying for allocation of State Board Issue funds to match funds from the Bureau of Vocational Rehabilitation shall follow the same procedures as for the allocation of construction and equipment funds.

Standard EDb-463-13

Special consideration may be given to any creative or exemplary cooperatively developed plan or plans to establish, maintain, and finance a comprehensive vocational education program for all eligible students through the granting of an exception to those standards which tend to inhibit the implementation of a plan which best serves the needs of students in such areas. Special consideration may also be given to one or more counties in which compliance with one or more of the standards would result in unreasonable transportation time and costs.

Standard EDb-463-14

In grant programs which support the provision of health, education or welfare services, discrimination in the selection or eligibility of individuals to receive the services, and segregation or other discriminatory practices in the manner of providing them, are prohibited. This prohibition extends to all facilities and services provided by the grantee under the program or, if the grantee is a State, by a political subdivision of the State. It extends also to services purchased or otherwise obtained by the grantee or political subdivision, and to the facilities in which such services are provided, subject, however, to the provisions of 80.3 (e). Sec. 602, Civil Rights Act of 1964, 78 Stat. 252; 42 U.S.C. 2000d-1

Standard EDb-463-15

Exemptions to the minimum requirement of 1,500 students in grades 9 through 12 may be made by the State Board of Education based on sparsity of population or other factors indicating that comprehensive educational and vocational programs can be provided through an alternate plan.

Note: Following adoption of the standards the State Board allocated $3,342,972 for constructing and equipping vocational education facilities to five Ohio school districts. The funds were the first to be allocated from the $75 million included in State Board Issue I approved by the citizens in November 1968.

Those districts that received funds were Alliance, $2,090,803; Bedford, $300,000; Lake County Joint Vocational School, 167,750; Northwest Local (Hamilton County), $276,640, and Toledo, $506,778. The five districts became eligible for construction and equipment funds after each submitted an approvable plan for vocational education as outlined in the new standards. Matching arrangements were available in each of the districts.

APPENDIX B

The First Ohio Council on Vocational Education Membership Roster

✦

(Appointed Under the Authority of Public Law 90-576)

Management:

Russell L. Bearss, Plant Manager, Chrysler Corporation
Jesse W. Fulton, General Office Manager, Addressograph-Multigraph Co.
Ray R. Runser, Director, Industrial Relations, Baldwin-Lima Hamilton Corp.

Labor:

Dr. Leo Dugan, Executive Secretary-Treasurer, Akron Labor Council, AFL-CIO
Frank King, President, Ohio AFL-CIO

State Industrial and Economic Development:

Fred Neuenschwander, Director, Ohio Department of Development

Higher Education:

Dr. George Bowers, Dean, School of Applied Science, Miami University
Dr. Max J. Lerner, President, Lorain Community College (Council Chair)
Charles Harbottle, President, Miami-Jacobs Junior College of Business

Administration of State and Local Vocational Programs:

William Mason, Past Director of Vocational Education, Cleveland City Schools

Dr. Robert Reese, Professor, Vocational Education, The Ohio State University

Vocational and Technical Programs:

Robert Durbin, Superintendent, Four County Joint Vocational School

R. A. Guinn, Director, Vocational Education, Marietta City Schools

Local Boards of Education:

Mrs. James Shellabarger, Member, Dayton City Board of Education

Manpower Agencies:

William Papier, Director, Research & Statistics, Ohio Bureau of Employment Services

School Systems with Concentrations of Disadvantaged Students:

Dr. Paul Miller, Superintendent, Cincinnati City Schools

Knowledge of Programs for Students with Special Needs:

Mrs. Harold F. Bannister, Executive Director, Vocational Guidance & Rehabilitation Services, Cleveland

General Public:

Hugh Frost, Assistant to the President, Youngstown State University

Joseph A. Hall, Director, Urban League of Greater Cincinnati

Agriculture:

Dean Simeral, Associate Director for Public Affairs, Ohio Farm Bureau Federation

Distribution:

Karl Kahler, Executive Director, Ohio State Council for Retail Merchants

Parents and Teachers Association (PTA):

Mrs. Dale M. Corrigan, Director, Ohio Congress of Parents and Teachers

APPENDIX C

Joint Vocational School Districts

Apollo
Ashland County-Ashtabula
Auburn
Belmont-Harrison
Buckeye
Butler County
Columbiana County
Coshocton County
Cuyahoga Valley
Delaware County
Eastland-Fairfield
EHOVE
Central Ohio
Four County
Gallia-Jackson-Vinton
Great Oaks
Greene County
Jefferson County
Knox County
Lawrence County
Licking County (C-TEC)
Lorain County
Mahoning County
Maplewood
Medina County

Miami Valley
Mid-East Ohio
Ohio Hi-Point
Penta County
Pickaway-Ross
Pike County
Pioneer
Polaris
Portage Lakes
Scioto County
Southern Hills
Springfield Clark County
Stark County
Tri-County
Tri-Rivers
Trumbull County
U. S. Grant
West Holmes
Upper Valley
Vanguard
Vantage
Warren County
Washington County
Wayne County

APPENDIX D

Comprehensive/Contract Career Technical Planning Districts

Akron City
Alliance City
Bedford-Maple Heights City
Canton City
Canton Local
Centerville City
Cincinnati City
Cleveland Municipal
Columbus City
Dayton City
East Cleveland City
East Liverpool City
Four Cities Educational Compact
Greenville City
Hamilton City
Lake Shore Compact
Lancaster City
Lima City
Lorain City
Mad River Local
Madison Local
Mansfield City

Massillon City
Mayfield Excel
Meigs Local
Millstream
Morgan Local
Northwest Local
Ohio Central School System
Ohio Department of Youth Services
Ohio Valley Local Oregon City
Parma City
Plain Local
Sandusky City
Six District Educational Compact
South-Western City
Switzerland of Ohio Local
Sylvania City
Toledo City
Tri-Heights Career Prep Consortium
Tri-Star Career Compact
Washington Local
West Shore Compact
Youngstown City

APPENDIX E

A Philosophy for Vocational Education

by Byrl R. Shoemaker
Director of Vocational Education
State Department of Education
Columbus, Ohio
1975

1.0 Background

1.1 A philosophy of education must provide a reason for the structure and program of education offered or serve as a stimulus for educational change. A philosophy for vocational education must provide answers to such questions as:

1.11 Why should vocational education be offered as a part of the public education effort for youth and adults? What are the social bases, the economic reasons and the educational factors?

1.12 Who should be served by the vocational education programs?

1.13 What should be the nature of the organization, scope and content of vocational education programs?

The overall purpose of education in any society is to prepare people to perpetuate and improve the society in which they live. An educational program in any nation must be related to the political, social and economic patterns within the nation.

2.0 Philosophy Statement

2.1 <u>The nature of work in our technological society requires formal preparation for entrance into the work force. Vocational education, therefore, must be a significant part of the educational system in our society.</u>

Educational programs in any nation must be related to the political, social and economic patterns within the nation. An overall purpose of education in any society can be stated, "the purpose of a public education program is to prepare people to adjust to and improve the society in which it exists". The educational process, therefore, is constantly affected by the society in which it exists and by the social and economic factors prevailing in that society. Early efforts in education within our nation emphasized the importance of literacy and citizenship training, since a republic depends upon a literate, informed and concerned citizenry.

As our society grew more affluent, more complex, free public education was extended upwards into the high school years. At the time the early high schools were organized the large majority of youth attending high school did so as a preparation for attending college. Job skills, other than the professions, were learned by a pass-on procedure of father to son, through a process of apprenticeship, indenture, or through the pickup process.

Today the jobs available are not apparent to youth or adults. Only 4.7% of the jobs within that society are unskilled and only 12.6% of the jobs in that society requires a baccalaureate degree. The nature of the economy and nature of the work have limited the opportunities for apprenticeship or through learning by the pickup process.

2.2 <u>Vocational education is essential for and must relate to the productivity of people, not only in competence related to an occupation, but in the attitude towards that occupation and a willingness to produce.</u>

Studies by the Brookings Institute reflect the economic significance imbedded within the vocational education curriculum. Such studies indicate that while the United States was number one in growth-rate real output per man-hour for many years during the growth pattern within our nation, we no longer enjoy that ranking for economic superiority. These studies also indicate that the United States is dead last among the developed nations of the world in growth-rate real output per man-hour. Japan is number one; West Germany is number two, and the United States of America is number 20.

Additional studies with regard to the factors relating to "growth-rate real output per man-hour" indicate that such growth-rate is made up of 15% machines, 36% knowledge related to production, 42% education and 7% miscellaneous. A synthesis of these factors suggest that our competitive capability, therefore, is related to the education of our employment base, and vocational education is dedicated to improving the productivity of our work force.

2.3 <u>The uniqueness of vocational education is the preparation for work which permeates the vocational programs at both the high school and post-high school level.</u>

Vocational education cannot be classified as a unique discipline within the educational system. Rather, it can be identified as a program in which we combine the skills and technical content of various disciplines with the practical requirements of the world of work in order to prepare a young person to succeed technically and socially in world of work. Vocational education, while not unique as a discipline, is unique as a program and this uniqueness is reflected in facilities and equipment needed for the instructional program, curriculums, instructor qualifications and student goals and services.

Since employability is the goal of vocational education the program must make contributions to the development on the part of the students enrolled of citizenship qualities, work habits and attitudes, safety judgments, understanding of occupational choice and other factors common to many elements of other educational programs. Compatible skills of communication, decision-making, learning to learn and personal and occupational responsibility are equally important and equally within the purvey of vocational education. These "true salable skills", and the individual's capacity to transfer them regularly and usefully to his/her work and life needs throughout life, require that vocational education emphasize the development of such conceptions.

Vocational education has an excellent opportunity to instruct in such common learnings. If vocational education programs, however, do not maintain the uniqueness of preparation for work which is not found in any other educational program, it is questionable as to whether the added costs of vocational education justify the offering of the program for instruction which could be gained in other programs of learning.

2.4 <u>Vocational education programs must be available for your 16 years of age and older at both the high school and post-high school levels and for adults throughout the work life of the individual.</u>

Instruction within vocational education programs must be compatible with educational theory and principles of learning growing out of research in psychology and education.

Decisions relating to the starting point for vocational education within the educational program for youth and adults must relate to the studies on child development and occupational choice. Studies in guidance relating to occupational choice indicate that a young person's occupational choice becomes reasonable at age 16 if they are provided education for choice. Observations not yet substantiated by research suggest that psychologically youth become goal-oriented at age 16 and any mandatory educational program at that age or beyond must relate to such goals. It is a fact for the majority of youth that high school is their last chance for a full-time educational program. It is also clear that a number of youth want to delay or have their first opportunity for vocational education after they leave high school.

The rapid changes in occupations and the needs of adults for retraining and upgrading instruction throughout their work life point up the need for facilities and programs to serve the needs of youth and adults in all areas of education in the nation.

2.5 <u>Vocational education is an important part of the educational program, and the nature and quantity of vocational education must be in keeping with employment patterns and trends locally, state and nationally, in that order.</u>

Every set of objectives, including the "seven cardinal principles of education", "the ten imperative needs of youth", developed by a national principals' group or the "developmental needs of youth", as identified by Havighurst, all establish the importance of preparing youth who are not going on to college for employment. Emphasis in education, both at the high school and collegiate level, however, has essentially focused on a subject-centered college preparatory curriculum at the high school level and subject-centered professional curriculum at the collegiate level. Research pointing to the lack of correlation of success of the college preparatory program in relation to success in college raises serious questions about such an approach. Only in recent years have significant developments been made in both high school and post-high school vocational and technical education, preparing youth for employment in occupations other then professions.

The needs of the individual and the society, the technological developments within our nation, the basis for our competition within the world markets, research within education regarding the learning process, and the overall purposes of education within any society would lead planners in the field of education to include preparation for both paid and non-paid work as one of the significant goals of the educational process.

In taking a position of significance in the educational system, vocational education must recognize and address the rising rate of permanent unemployment, the increasing rate of job change and the continually changing nature of most jobs.

2.6 <u>Both the competencies and the interests of the individual must be considered, but the opportunities within and needs of society in which the individual will participate must be considered as vocational education programs are established.</u>

A philosophy for vocational education must grow out of and be in harmony with a total philosophy of education for the individual and/or the society in which he lives and works. The importance of the individual within an educational program is without question. Some philosophers, such as Socrates, have made the concern for an individual the all-important factor within their philosophy. Other philosophers, such as Aristotle and Georg Wilhelm Friedrich Hegel, who came after Socrates, saw man as a social being who could find his identity or reality only in the State.

Interests of the individual must be considered in establishing a vocational program, but employment trends must indicate a good chance for employment of graduates from such vocational programs.

2.7 <u>Instruction within vocational education programs must be compatible with educational theory and principles of learning growing out of research in psychology and education.</u>

A study of the learning process itself will show that the early philosophers in education such as Rousseau, Pestalozzi and Froebel, all saw the need for the inclusion of student experiences within education. Psychology of learning provided a research base to prove many of the concepts of the early philosophers. Principles of learning growing out of these psychological studies were stated by Gerald Leighbody as follows:

> *We learn best when we are ready to learn. When we have a strong purpose, a well-fixed reason for learning something, it is easier to receive the instruction and to make progress in learning.*
>
> *The more often we use what we have learning the better we can perform or understand it.*
>
> *If the things we have learned are useful and beneficial to us so that we are satisfied with what we have accomplished, the better we retain what we have learned.*
>
> *Learning something new is made easier if the learning can be built upon something we already know. It is best to start with simple steps which are related to things we can now do or which we already understand and progress to new and more difficult tasks or ideas.*
>
> *Learning takes place by doing. Before the learning can become complete, we must put into practice what we are attempting to learn.*

The principles for vocational education outlined by Prosser apply learning theory and results of psychological studies on learning to programs of vocational education.

2.8 Vocational programming requires a time commitment of sufficient length and intensity to provide instruction in the several domains important to the successful entrance of the student into and their progress within the occupation of their choice.

A sound vocational education program must be concerned with the employability of the student upon completion of the vocational program and with the ability of that student to adjust to technical changes within that occupation and changes in the social setting of the occupation. The curriculum for vocational education, therefore, must be concerned with and provide instructional experiences relating to the psychomotor, the cognitive, the affective and the perceptive domains as they relate to preparing the student for employability. Since the unique role of vocational education is preparation for employment, the physical facilities and equipment, qualification of the instructional staff, the organization of the curriculum and the recruitment, enrollment and placement of the students must all reflect the unique role of vocational education within the curriculum as well as the commitment of vocational education to the common learnings demanded of every educational program.

Vocational education is a program and adequate time must be provided for the learner to gain the skills, technical knowledge, social attitudes and competencies essential for entrance into or progress in employment.

2.9 <u>An effective vocational education program requires competency in reading, writing and arithmetic and experiences leading to a sound occupational choice.</u>

There are no semi-skilled, skilled or technical occupations which do not require literacy in terms of the basic skills of reading, writing and arithmetic. If such skills are not present when a student enrolls in a vocational program, they must be taught concurrently with the skills of an occupation.

An individual can likely be successful in several different occupations. Each person, therefore, must be provided experiences prior to enrollment in vocational education which: motivate them to want to work and to respect all work; orient them to the various semi-skilled, skilled, technical and professional occupations available in the work force; and give them the opportunity to explore selected occupations to determine their interests and capabilities.

3.0 Summary

3.1 <u>Vocational education programs, based upon the principles outlined, must be provided for all eligible age levels, all ability levels, in all sections of a state and the nation. Programs must be occupationally based and designed to meet the needs of both an individual and the society in which he exists. Vocational education starts with the job and ends with the student successfully employed on the job.</u>

APPENDIX F

Standard Characteristics of Vocational Education

by Darrell L. Parks
Assistant Director, Vocational Education
Department of Education
Columbus, Ohio ACTE

Presented at the 1975 National Leadership Development Seminar
for State Directors of Vocational Education

"Issues and Answers in Vocational Education"

September 23-26, 1975
The Wildwood Inn—Snowmass, Colorado

To discuss standard characteristics of vocational education apart from the philosophy and definition is a very difficult task. Standard characteristics should be:

- an outgrowth of a philosophy of vocational education,
- consistent with the role of vocational education,
- a corporate part of the governance of vocational education, and
- supportive to the definition of vocational education.

Thus, the standard characteristics of vocational education, as set forth in this paper, will by necessity reflect and relate to a philosophy and definition. Furthermore, the term "standard characteristics", as reflected within the context of this paper, relates to distinguishing traits or features regarding vocational education which are important in fulfilling its purpose, and which may or may not be consistent with individual educational disciplines.

For the purpose of this paper, standard characteristics of vocational education will be viewed from a perspective common to both state and local levels of program administration an/or operation. Admittedly, selected characteristics may have slightly different interpretations depending on the program level. However, the ensuing proposed characteristics are inherent to sound program management and effective services to youth and adults regardless of the level of operation.

1. **Philosophical and educational foundation**:

Initially a program of vocational education must be founded upon a sound philosophical and educational base. Without such a base upon which to build, the program will have neither stability nor a sense of direction.

The program philosophy should reflect the fundamental purpose of vocational education and its place in the social, economic and educational environments. Specifically, the philosophy should address two fundamental questions:

a. Why vocational education in lieu of or in conjunction with other educational concepts?

b. What is vocational education with respect to meeting current and projected social, economic and individual needs?

The educational program should be a core type curriculum aimed at preparing individuals for employment. Such a vocational education base must embrace the principles of learning which point up the importance of the relationship of knowledge taught to the effective use and application of such knowledge.

The philosophical and educational foundation for vocational education must emanate from a state leadership point of view. However, such a foundation must be subscribed to at the local level of program administration and operation if it is to be effective.

Subsequent to the formulating of a philosophical and educational base relative to vocational education, it is necessary to structure and implement an effective delivery system for vocational education. Such a delivery system must possess a set of standard characteristics if the state educational agency (SEA) and the local educational agencies (LEA) are to fulfill their respective leadership roles in program development, implementation and administration.

2. Constituency support

Although treated as a separate entity, building program constituency is dependent upon and closely allied with other characteristics related to program philosophy, quality and outcomes. However, the importance of program constituency merits discussing it independently of other common characteristics.

Constituency support does not come about automatically, but must be cultivated and nurtured at all program levels if vocational education is to prosper and grow. Vocational education is a service effort for both the individual and business industry. Close relationships must be developed and maintained with persons who need vocational education and agencies who employ the product in order to assure current and relevant program content and skill development. Vocational education functions within, and as a part of the social and economic environment. Community involvement and input must be sought and taken into account if continuing public support is to be realized. Legislatively, there must be laws and regulations and financial support for vocational education if it is to reach its potential in services to our society, and finally, vocational education must be packaged in such a manner that it appeals to the needs and interests of a significant segment of the student clientele.

Ultimately, the goal of building a constituency is to attain the degree of commitment and support for vocational education that will assure its prominence and permanence on the educational scene. <u>Thus, each program level and, in fact, each individual program offering, must possess and effectively utilize the appropriate constituency promoting vehicles essential to program development, operation and success.</u>

3. Program planning

It is the responsibility of the SEA to provide an adequate program of vocational education for all people in all parts of the state. In order to fulfill such a responsibility, careful and detailed planning on a statewide basis is essential. Such planning must be based upon a set of statewide goals and measurable program objectives and the effective utilization of valid regional and/or statewide data and information.

Once developed, the state plan for vocational education must be translated into LEA level plans of action. If differences arise between SEA and LEA plans of action for vocational education, adjustments will have to be effected in order that plans are compatible. Hence, a standard characteristic of vocational education at all program levels should be a carefully developed and documented program plan that is based upon a set of specific goals and measurable program objectives and which will facilitate and support planning and programming efforts.

4. Pattern for program development and expansion

Like most social movements supported and financed via local, state and/or federal tax revenues, vocational education must compete for the limited tax dollar. Based on the assumption that vocational education needs exceed available sources of revenue, it is essential that optimal use be made of available dollars. The assurance that fiscal optimization is being realized necessitates a carefully derived pattern for program development and expansion. Thus, a fourth standard characteristic of vocational education should be the existence of a comprehensive pattern for program development and expansion supported by legislation and fiscal commitments at the state and local levels, and which takes into account occupational needs, student base, and educational resources available or required.

5. Program standards

In order to provide the quality of services needed by the individual and employers and to assure an effective use of fiscal and educational resources throughout the state, it is essential that vocational education programs be built around and maintained upon a set of appropriate program standards. These standards should address the "four factors of production" relative to vocational education, namely; curriculum and instruction, facilities and equipment, instructional staff and students. Consequently, a fifth standard characteristic of vocational education should be the availability of a comprehensive set of program standards related to the "four factors of production" in vocational education that contribute to and enhance the quality of the programs of instruction. Such standards must be accompanied by the appropriate mechanisms for monitoring and enforcing the.

6. Personnel development

Regardless of the soundness of the program philosophy, the comprehensiveness of goals and objectives, or the appropriateness of program standards, the degree to which vocational education is effective is largely dependent upon the availability of quality state and local leadership and instructional personnel. A supply of competent personnel is too important to vocational education's success to leave to chance. Thus, a sixth standard characteristic of vocational education should be a well defined and operative program of professional personnel development which assures an adequate supply of leadership and instructional personnel who are imbued with both the technical and pedagogical skills and understandings essential to program development and operation.

7. Evaluation

Program review and evaluation are key ingredients to any program's success. Program review in vocational education should embrace two dimensions; namely, process and product evaluation.

Process evaluation is formative in nature and its primary purpose should be the improvement, development and expansion of vocational education. This evaluative component assures the effectiveness of the program variables of curriculum and instruction, facilities and equipment, instructional staff and students. Comprehensive evaluation measures of a formative nature should provide for a self-review of programs at the operational level as well as an external assessment from a SEA perspective.

The degree of success and support enjoyed by vocational education will be largely dependent upon the number of students who obtain full time employment and who perform satisfactorily on the job. Such employment obtained by the products of vocational education must be directly related or closely associated to the type of training received. Student placement and follow-up is essentially a product or summative evaluation component and is the accountability measure for vocational education. Placement and follow-up evaluation is primarily a LEA responsibility and not only reflects the qualitative aspects of the educational program, but also assesses the soundness of the philosophical and educational base upon which the program has been built.

Therefore, an inherent standard characteristic of vocational education is a mechanism which provides for periodic formative and summative program evaluation. It is desirable that such a review process include a LEA self-review and an external review from a SEA level. The evaluation mechanism should also provide a means for review follow-up and program redirection.

In summary, standard characteristics of vocational education must be an outgrowth of and built upon a philosophical foundation. Once the standard characteristics have been determined, operational criteria must be established for each standard characteristic. The establishing of such operational criteria must once again evolve from and relate to the program philosophy.

APPENDIX G

A Roster of State Vocational Education Leadership in Ohio

✦

1920-2006

State Directors		Term of Service
C. H. Brady		1920-1921
Joseph Stroebel		1944-1950
Ralph Howard		1950-1962
Byrl R. Shoemaker		1962-1982
Darrell L. Parks		1982-1995
Joanna Kister		1995-2000
Vicki Melvin		2000-2005
Kathy Shibley		2006-present

Associate Directors	Title	
Jim Bowling	Adult Learning Services	2001-present
Thomas Applegate	Business, Industry & Interagency Linkages	1992-1997
Sonia Price	Curriculum & Instruction	1986-1990
Vicki Melvin	Curriculum & Instruction	1990-2005
James Pinchak	Planning & Program Services	1986-1996

Associate Directors	*Title*	
Kathy Shibley	Pathway, Programs & Services	2005-2006
Rick Mangini	Pathway, Programs & Services	2006-present
Charlotte Coomer	System Planning, Analysis& Improvement	1991-2002
Linnae Clinton	System Planning, Analysis& Improvement	2002-2005
Raul Soto	System Planning, Analysis& Improvement	2006-present

Assistant Directors

1. Administration

D. Ray Purkey	1970-1972
Darrell L. Parks	1972
George Kosbab	1972-1977

2. Planning & Administrative Services (Research Coordinating Unit)

C. O Tower	1964-1969
Robert D. Balthaser	1969-1986
James G Pinchak	1986-1996
Robert D. Sommers	1996-2001

3. Curriculum & Professional Development

Darrell L. Parks	1970-1971
Robert Koon	1971-1975
Darrell L. Parks	1975-1978
George Kosbab	1978-1982

4. Construction & Equipment

D. Ray Purkey	1966-1970
Frank Oliverio	1970-1983

5. Agricultural Education

Ray Fife	1917-1936
Ralph Howard	1936-1950
Warren Weiler	1950-1969
James E. Dougan	1969-1979
Darrell L. Parks	1979-1982
James E. Cummins	1982-1987
John Davis	1987-1992
Robert D. Sommers	1992-1996
Isaac Kershaw	1996-present

6. Business & Office Education (Business, Marketing & Information Technology)

Robert D. Balthaser	1957-1969
Donald Potter	1969-1972
Ted R. Johnson	1972-1976
Dan Viceral	1976-1982
Larry Casterline	1982-1990
Rick Mangini	1990-2006

7. Distributive Education

Marguerite Loos	1938-1963
Bernard Nye	1963-1984

8. Home Economics (Family & Consumer Sciences)

Treva E. Kaufman	1918-1921
Maude Adams	1921
Enid Lunn	1921-1958

Margaret McEniry	1958-1969
Sonia Price	1969-1982
Joanna Kister	1982-1995
Dee Allenspach	1995-1998
Sharon Enright	1998-2005
Leslie Brady	2005-present

9. Trade & Industrial Education

Albert E. Heusch	1917-1945
Robert Reese	1945-1956
Byrl Shoemaker	1956-1962
Earl Fowler	1962
Harry Davis	1962-1982
James Wiblin	1982-1997
Bob Bowermeister	1997-2003
Kathy Sommers	2003-present

10. Special Needs

Hebert Brum	1967-1970
Richard Macer	1970-1988
James Gifreda	1988-1991

11. Career Education/OCIS

Jack Ford	1970-1979
Karen Shylo	1979-1986
Karen Heath	1986-1998
James Cummins	1998-2000
Cindi Gahris	2000-present

12. Guidance

John Odgers	1946-1958

(In 1958, Guidance was established as a separate division within the Department of Education.)

13. Veterans Training

Ernie Shaffer	1945-1946
Lawrence Borosage	1946-1947
Helen Ward	1947-1954
Bernard Miller	1954-1955
Robert Chandler	1955-1961
Robert Guyton	1961-1971
Robert Wientjes	1978-1985
Clark DeVol	1985-1991
Claudia Jones	1991-present

14. Manpower Development & Training (CETA, JTPA)

Steve Stuart	1962-1964
James Noel	1964-1978
Ivan Winland	1978-1985
Pat Doerman	1985-1986
Vicki Melvin	1986-1990
Kristen Cox	1990-present

Executive Secretaries/State Advisors, Vocational Student Organizations

1. Office Education Association (OEA, Business Professionals of America)

Donald Potter	1967-1971

William Dross	1971-1987
Charlotte Coomer	1987-1991
Rick Mangini	1991-present

2. Distributive Education Clubs of America (DECA)

Amanda Thomas	1940s
(Records between the 1940s and 1967 were unavailable.)	
Leon Linton	1967-1969
Gary Pozik	1969-1970
J.W. Weatherford	1970-1972
David Rankin	1972-1985
Jim Price	1985-1989
Rick Mangini	1989-present

3. Future Farmers of America (FFA)

Ralph Howard	1929-1937
Warren Weiler	1937-1950
D. Ray Purkey	1950-1963
Earl F. Kantner	1963-1984
Robin Hovis	1984-1988
James Scott	1988-1995
Steve Gratz	1995-present

4. Future Homemakers of America (FHA/HERO)

Margaret McEniry	1958-1965
Dorothy Foster	1965-1968
Adele Reagle	1968-1991
Marjorie Hines	1992-1994

Carol Whitmore	1994-2000
Vicky Warner	2000-2002
Rick Mangini	2003-2005
(Bonnie Hansen—Ohio FCCLA State Coordinator)	2001-2003
(Bonnie Ayars—Ohio FCCLA State Coordinator)	2004-(six months)
(Paulette Farago—Ohio FCCLA State Coordinator)	2004-2005
Paulette Farago	2005-present

5. Vocational Industrial Clubs of America (VICA)

Byrl Shoemaker	1952-1955
Carl Shaefer	1955-1961
Merle Strong	1961-1964
Ralph Neal	1964-1966
Charles Dygert	1966-1979
Robert Whisman	1979-1986
Jeff Merickel	1986-2001
Mike Cowles	2001-present

6. Jobs for Ohio Graduates (JOG)

| Lee Blanton | 1986-2003 |

(In 2003, JOG, Inc. became an independent, non-profit organization, supported by federal Worker Investment Act (WIA) funds and state dollars appropriated by the Ohio General Assembly. Lee Blanton continues in a state JOG leadership role with the title of chief executive officer.)

Postscript

Career, technical and adult education in Ohio is a work in progress. While history will acknowledge its evolution as perhaps the most significant educational reform movement in the 20th century, the program is still in a state of metamorphosis, adjusting to and accommodating the needs of an ever-changing state and national economic and social climate.

Some of its critics have asserted that the key to the economic success of this nation is for everyone to achieve a traditional four-year college degree. Others would suggest that career and technical education is a dead-end street that limits individual potential for job advancement and financial reward.

Nothing could be further from the truth. As our economy and our society move to an ever more sophisticated high-tech environment, the need for highly skilled knowledge workers will accelerate exponentially. And where will these knowledge workers come from?

Career and technical education is a proven and strategically positioned enterprise to respond to that need. It has established itself as a significant player in the public educational arena, and it is an in-place statewide system of state-of-the-art educational and training facilities with talented and dedicated professional staff and administrators.

Career/technical and adult education has proven its capacity to change rapidly to address the immediate and emerging employment and economic needs of Ohio's business and industrial community. It transitioned from a <u>hands-on</u> to a <u>head and hands-on</u> delivery system when it became apparent that literacy and academic skills went hand-in-hand with job skills in today's employment market.

Career and technical education, more than any other public education endeavor, is a proven equal education opportunity enterprise, offering a full range of programming and support services to all individuals regardless of age, race, sex, physical or mental limitation, or national origin.

But it cannot rest on its laurels.

Bibliography

A Report of the Governor's Task Force on Vocational and Technical Education (State of Ohio, 1969).

Amendments to the Vocational Education Act of 1963. Public Law 90-576, 90th Congress, HR 18366, October 16, 1968.

Carl D. Perkins Vocational Education Act. Public Law 98-524, 98th Congress, H.R. 4164, October 19, 1984.

Carl D. Perkins Vocational and Applied Technology Education Act Amendments of 1990. Public Law 101-392, 101st Congress, H.R. 7, September 25, 1990

Carl D. Perkins Vocational and Applied Technology Education Amendments of 1998. Public Law 105-332, 105th Congress, H.R. 2853, October 31, 1998.

Davis, Joseph L., *Vocational Education in Ohio: A 20th Century Story,* unpublished history of vocational education in Ohio, 1997.

Dempsey, Karen, *OWE Occupational Work Experience History: 1962-1982,* unpublished document with Foreword written by Dr. Thomas Hyde, State Coordinator of OWE Programs, Ohio Department of Education, Division of Vocational Education, May 2, 1982.

Education Amendments of 1976. Public Law 94-482, 94th Congress, S. 2657, October 12, 1976.

FY 95 Comprehensive Annual Performance Report to the United States Department of Education, Ohio Department of Education, Columbus.

Gordon, Howard R. D., *The History and Growth of Vocational Education in America,* Allyn & Bacon, Boston, 1999, 204 pp.

Highlights of State Statutes Concerning Vocational Education in Ohio (unpublished document), Ohio Department of Education, Division of Vocational and Career Education, January 1989.

History of Ohio's County Boards of Education, 1914-1989, Ohio Department of Education, Columbus, 1989, 143 pp.

Johnston, Richard E., The *History of Trade and Industrial Education in Ohio,* unpublished doctoral dissertation, The Ohio State University, 1971, 300 pp.

Learning a Living—A Blueprint for High Performance—A SCANS Report for America 2000, the Secretary's Commission for Achieving Necessary Skills, U. S. Department of Labor, April, 1992, 88 pp.

Milestones: A History of the State Board of Education in Ohio, 1956-1989, State Board of Education, Columbus, 1989, 107 pp.

Ohio Career-Technical and Adult Education Dictionary, Ohio Department of Education, Columbus, October 2004, pp.7-9.

Ohio Council on Vocational Education Annual Reports, 1971-1998. Ohio Department of Education, Columbus.

Ohio Department of Education Newsletter, Columbus, Number 275, February 1970.

Ohio's Future at Work, Ohio Department of Education, Division of Vocational Education, Columbus, June 1990, 32 pp.

Ohio's Future at Work: Beyond 2000, Ohio Department of Education, Office of Career-Technical and Adult Education, undated, 27 pp.

Ohio Legislation Applicable to Vocational Education With opinions of the Attorney General, Columbus, published by the Vocational Instructional Materials Laboratory, The Ohio State University, 1973.

Pinchak, G. J., *Factors Related to the Job Satisfaction of Teacher Coordinators in the Occupational Work Adjustment Program in Ohio,* unpublished doctoral dissertation, Bowling Green State University, 1982.

Roediger, Roger D., *A History of the Ohio Vocational Association,* Ohio Vocational Association, Columbus, 1961, 61 pp.

Rhodes, James A., *Alternative To A Decadent Society,* Indiana, Howard W. Sams & Co., Inc., 1969, 108 pp.

Rhodes, James A., *Vocational Education and Guidance*: A System for the Seventies Columbus, Charles E. Merrill Publishing, 1970, 163 pp.

Scott, John L. and Michelle Sarkees-Wircenski, *Overview of Vocational & Applied Technology Education,* American Technical Publishers, Inc., Homewood, IL, 1996, 258 pp.

Swanson, J. Chester, *Development of Federal Legislation for Vocational Education,* unpublished paper, 89 pp.

The Ohio Revised Code. Sections 3311.16, 3311.17, 3311.18, 3311.19, 3313.90

The Vocational Education Act of 1963, Public Law 88-210, 88th Congress, H.R. 4955, December 18, 1963.

Vocational Education, The Bridge Between Man and His Work, U.S. Department of Health, Education and Welfare, Washington, DC, Government Printing Office, 1968.

Vocational-Technical Education: Major Reforms and Debates 1917-Present, U.S. Department of Education, Office of Vocational and Adult Education, 1993, 30 pp.

Weiler, Warren G. and Ralph J. Woodin, *A History of the Ohio Vocational Agriculture Teachers Association—1925-1975,* Columbus, OH, Agricultural Education Curriculum Materials Service, The Ohio State University, 1975, 199 pp.

978-0-595-42497-9
0-595-42497-X

Printed in the United States
86210LV00008B/101/A